Safe Harbors
That Can
Reduce Taxes,
Remove Risk, and
Protect Your Retirement

**A Guide for Retirees
and
Those Contemplating Retirement**

Second Edition

by

Stephen J. Kelley, CSA®

Published By
Safety First Financial Planners
33 Main Street, Suite 201
Nashua, NH 03064
Tel: 603-881-8811 · Fax: 603-386-6080
mail@Safety1stFP.com · www.Safety1stFP.com
Also available online

Disclaimer and Copyright Information

No part of this book should be construed as financial, legal or accounting advice. You should not act on the concepts in this book without the help of a competent professional advisor. Illustrations are deemed accurate based on historical performance, however past performance is no guarantee of future results. Any numbers used in the calculators and illustrations within this book are deemed accurate but are for illustration purposes only.

Standard & Poor's®, S&P®, and S&P 500®, are registered trademarks of the McGraw-Hill Companies, Inc. The Russell 2000® Index is a registered trademark of The Frank Russell Company. The Dow Jones Industrial Average®, and DJIA® are registered trademarks of Dow Jones and Co.

The products and strategies outlined in this book are not sponsored, endorsed, sold or promoted by McGraw-Hill, Standard & Poor's, the Frank Russell Company or Dow Jones and Co., and these companies make no representation regarding the advisability of investing in them.

IPA™ and Consolpro™ are trademarks of Consolpro, Inc. I4L Lifetime Income™ is a trademark of Senior Resources, NH.

Dedication and Style Note

Sometimes in this book I refer to "I" and "me."

That's me, the recorder (not necessarily the author) of these words, Stephen Kelley.

Other times I refer to "we" and "us."

That's Consolpro™, the group of professionals these narratives and principals are based upon, and the real authors of this book.

I wasn't around at the beginning, but have been for several years, and owe whatever success I've had in this business to them.

I have never met a more principled, honest or knowledgeable group of people. I am proud and honored to be part of it, and am proud to dedicate this book to them.

Thanks, members of the Consolpro™ team, for all you've done.

"The Best Casino In The World"

What if you heard about a "No-Lose Casino" where you could go and bet as much money as you wanted, but were guaranteed never to lose a dime? Think of it; every time you made a bet, if you won, you won, but if you lost, you didn't lose anything!

And what if that casino were licensed by your state government, rated by national rating organizations, and had over 200 years of proven performance for millions of satisfied customers behind it? And, what if, in the course of its history, not one of the many millions of satisfied customers who went there ever lost a dime?

There is only one catch: if you win, you only get to take one half your winnings. So, if you bet on roulette, for example, and your number comes up, instead of paying 32:1 it only pays 16:1. But, if your number doesn't come up, all of the chips you put down are returned to you. And you can just keep on letting it ride...

Now, what if your butcher, baker, neighborhood policeman, brother-in-law and Uncle Charlie...none of whom had even been to Vegas...all told you it was too good to be true?

But now you are in Vegas and standing right in front of the No-Lose Casino, watching happy people emerge with giant stacks of money. What are you going to do? Believe your brother-in-law and Uncle Charlie, or go in and find out what is happening that's making all of these people so happy? Wouldn't you at least investigate...get more information, and find out if it was true or not?

Well now's your chance. That casino doesn't really exist, but there is something very similar to it in the retirement planning world that allows you to win when the market goes up, but protects all your principal and gains when it goes down.

That's one of the things this book is about. Keep reading. Maybe you'll be able to teach your Uncle Charlie a thing or two...not to mention your brother-in-law. How sweet would that be?

Table of Contents

When you are young and accumulating, time works in your favor because the overall trend in the market is historically upwards. However as you age the time you have to recover from a loss is much shorter. Time is now the enemy, so risk becomes much more dangerous than when you were young.

-Page 6

Unfortunately, it is during this time the lawyers and the courts are earning their fees...One lawyer friend of mine calls probate his ARP (Attorney Retirement Plan).

-Page 19

Bogle continued: "Think about that. That means <u>the financial system put up zero percent of the capital and took zero percent of the risk and got almost 80 percent of the return</u>. And you...put up 100 percent of the capital, took 100 percent of the risk, and got only a little bit over 20 percent of the return."

-Page 33

An ugly truth the industry doesn't want you to know is that the average equity investor has earned just 2.7% per year since 1984.

-Page 34

In fact, they may be the safest accounts in history. It's the truth: during the depression when banks were failing and people couldn't get their money, where did they turn? You guessed it—life insurance and fixed annuities!

-Page 68

... Ben Bernanke, Chairman of the Federal Reserve, is said to hold 100% of his retirement in annuities.

-Page 69

It is truly amazing to see the kinds of things we can do for people once risk, unnecessary fees, and taxes are taken out of the equation. We have helped people recoup losses and build solid financial futures with guaranteed income and security without the guesswork. If you have a better way...anywhere...take it.

-Page 81

But what if there was a way? What if you could put your money in a very safe place...one that guaranteed you would never lose your principal or accrued interest? One that automatically "bought low" and "sold high"? ...One that was tax-deferred and free of fees? One that returned all of your principal and earnings in the case of emergencies, death, etc., and provided excellent annual liquidity, penalty free? Further, one that could provide income guarantees for the rest of your life, ensuring up to 60% more income than could be had from any equity markets?

-Page 84

,

Affiliations & Certifications

 The National Ethics Bureau (NEB) is an organization that provides services similar to the Better Business Bureau (BBB). However, NEB has an extensive nationwide background check process designed specifically for financial professionals. Mr. Kelley is proud to be a member of and support this fine organization. To maintain membership, financial professionals must undergo the following every year.

- Criminal Background Check – 7 Year
- Civil Background Check – 7 Year
- Professional License Check – 7 Year
- SEC (Securities and Exchange Commission) – 7 Year
- Bankruptcy Check – 7 Year
- Department of Insurance – 7 Year
- FINRA (Financial Industry Regulatory Authority) – 7 Year
- State Securities Administrators – 7 Year

 Ed Slott, CPA was named "The Best" source for IRA advice by The Wall Street Journal and called "America's IRA Expert" by Mutual Funds Magazine. He is a widely recognized professional speaker and created the nationally aired Public Television special, "Stay Rich Forever & Ever with Ed Slott." He has established Ed Slott's Elite IRA Advisor Group™, which was developed specifically to help financial institutions, financial advisors, firms and insurance companies become recognized leaders in the IRA marketplace. As a member of this organization, Mr. Kelley is a member of an elite group of advisors who receive extensive and ongoing training by Mr. Slott and his organization in the area of IRA planning.

 SCSA educates professionals to work more effectively with their senior clients so they will understand the key health, social and financial factors that are important to seniors—and how these factors work together. CSAs are able to integrate this into their professional practices, no matter what field they're in. Seniors can take an additional measure of confidence in the CSAs they're working with because the CSA certification program has met the 21 stringent standards necessary to earn NCCA accreditation. Also, many regulators believe that NCCA accreditation provides an added level of protection to seniors who may be unaware of what designations mean and what they represent.

Dear Reader,

Now that you are in or nearing retirement, it's a good time to take stock of what is really important to you during the years you have left. It could be providing for your grandchildren's education, leaving a family legacy, or ensuring that you have enough money to last you for the rest of your life. Or maybe you've always wanted to take your family on a cruise, or your grandchildren to Disney World. Whatever your goals, the information in this book may be of great help in achieving them.

Many retirees and seniors love to go on cruises. And why not? Everything you could possibly want or need is right there for you: first class service, wonderful food, beautiful accommodations, exciting entertainment, and exotic ports. Who could want more? Well there is one, very key thing, and that is calm seas.

Unfortunately, we live in a world with dynamic weather patterns. Storms can rise seemingly from nowhere and toss the ship as if it were a toy. In the same way, there are many economic and legal storms that can endanger your retirement.

However, with the help of good charts (your financial plan), a sound vessel (your life savings), a keen understanding of the financial climate, and a knowledge of how to find and utilize the Safe Harbors available to you along the way, your retirement can be a rewarding, safe, and marvelous adventure.

In 1933 Congress enacted the Securities Act of 1933, requiring for the first time that securities for sale within the United State be registered with the Federal Government (initially with the Federal Trade Commission), and then a year later, the Securities and Exchange Commission (SEC) was created pursuant to the Securities Exchange Act of 1934. Part of the initial Act of 1933 was Rule 151 which provided for a "Safe Harbor" provision for fixed annuities, thus exempting them from registration as securities as long as, among other things, <u>there were guarantees provided for principal and interest and all investment risk was born by the issuing insurance company.</u>

This is very important. Please read it again: <u>guarantees provided for principal and interest and all investment risk was born by the issuing insurance company.</u>

Over the years we have specialized in these and other no-risk, no-fee saving strategies, hence the title of the book.

I have had fun with the metaphor and with trying to fit all of the various things we do into these nautical terms. Please forgive me if I've gone a bit "overboard."

I hope you enjoy this little book. It represents several hundred hours of recapping our four decades of helping people just like you find the route to a secure retirement.

Even more, I hope that it helps you achieve those goals, needs and desires you've set out for yourself during your golden years. Many people have told us it did, and that has made it all worthwhile.

Bon Voyage!

Stephen Kelley

The Times, They Are A Changin'

Since the first printing of this book our world has been turned on its head. The old rules no longer apply (we have learned they really never did). People who thought they were ready to retire have either stayed in their jobs or gone back to work, when and where they could find it. Others who thought their jobs were secure have been cut loose and are now unemployed; some for the first time in their lives.

The market has crashed dramatically and people have lost as much as half or more of their wealth. Home values have declined for the first time in decades. Grand old companies like General Electric are on the skids. Others, like GM are in bankruptcy. The Federal Government has spent about $2 trillion to try to rectify the matter, and many believe there is much more to come.

But there is a broader change going on as well; one that has been going on for decades and that there likely will be no "recovery" from. For the first time in our history we are coming face to face with the limitations of our world.

During the 1970s, the deficit was $50 billion and the national debt was $1 trillion. Today's deficit is almost $2 trillion! The stimulus and bailout packages—as necessary as they may have been—have added to that mess. On top of that, the largest group of people in history are positioned to retire in the next 18 years, throwing further strain on the entire financial system.

According to the U.S. Census Bureau, the life expectancy of today's 75 year old was between 63 and 64 years old. Today the average 75 year old is expected to live another 10 years! Today's babies are being born with life expectancies of 80 years. If this trend continues, many, if not most, could live to be over 100!

In 1934 when Social Security was first established, the life expectancy of the average worker was 63 years old. Social Security was designed to kick in at age 65...two years after most people were expected to pass away. In those days people worked their whole lives, retired for a couple of years if they were fortunate, and then died. Today, at age 65, we as planners must consider the possibility of another quarter century of life...or even longer.

The designers of Social Security never intended it to be a retirement plan for decades the masses...it was intended to be a safety net for those who lived beyond standard life expectancy.

But that's just the beginning. Not only are people living longer, but there are more people as well. The 70-77 million baby boomers (those born between 1946-1964) are now beginning to retire and are expecting to collect Social Security. The first of the boomers began receiving payments in 2007, so we are just at the tip of this iceberg.

As you may or may not know, Social Security is a "pay as you go" system. There is no trust fund...that's a myth. Today's tax payers pay for today's beneficiaries. In 2005 the Congressional Budget Office predicted that outlays for Social Security will eclipse revenues by the year 2020.

And Social Security isn't the worst of it. Medicare and Medicaid are in even worst trouble...largely because of the same issues facing Social Security. In 2005 Douglas Holtz-Eakin, former director of the Congressional Budget Office, testified before Congress that by 2050 the cost of Medicare and Medicaid would expand to an amount equal to the current federal budget!

Who will pay all of these bills? Why the tax payer of course...you, me, our children, and their children.

Market Forces or Forced Markets?

For years, the market gurus have touted the benefits of investing in publicly traded securities, making the case that over time, the market always goes up. And over long periods of time this is often true. Especially during the period of time between 1972 and 1997, when the market grew at an average rate of 8.99% per year.

What happen to kick off this incredible period of expansion? In 1972 today's 401(k) was created. This caused billions of dollars to start flowing into the market; both the billions from employees and the matching funds from employers. In fact, according to the U.S. Census Bureau, over 80% of that money is tied to market performance. Think about it; trillions of dollars have poured into the market over the past 27 years, bidding up the prices of stocks and bonds. No wonder there was such growth during the latter part of the 20th Century.

Want more evidence? In 1972, the market traded 130 million shares in one day. In recent years, that number has reached nearly 12 billion shares! What happens when lots and lots of buyers are bidding on the same thing? Right. Prices go up!

However, at the end of 1997, the S&P 500 was at $970. Yesterday's market close was $888. That means in the past 12 years it has lost almost 10% of its value. What has happened? Well, lots of things; many of them covered in this forward. But what about the inevitable recovery everyone (including, probably, your advisor) is insisting is just around the corner? It *has* to go back up...right?

In 2007 the first Baby Boomer retired. That means that over the next 18 years, 70 million people will be retiring. As that happens, what happens to their contributions in the market? At the very best, they stop. At worst, trillions of dollars will be pulled out to support these people during their retirement, compounding the trillions already lost to the recent economic downturn.

What's that fact do to the argument that the market "has to come back?"

3

My opinion, and that of those whose opinions I respect, is that all bets are off. In spite of the recent gains I don't expect to see the market roaring back anytime soon. And I think that anyone who is betting on the market returning to its previous highs is taking a sucker's bet.

"But what about the recent rebound?" people often ask me. "Doesn't that prove that the market is coming back?"

I say...great...you are only down 20% instead of 40%. Now would be a great time to get out and lessen the damage. See, the only way to lock in a position is to sell. You didn't sell at the high...why not? So why not sell now, lock in your position, and move to an instrument where you can accumulate without getting hurt? So much better to lock in your gains every year...and that's just what Safe Harbor Fixed Annuities do!

Many experts believe we haven't yet seen the bottom. As the economy worsens and people continue to take money out of the market in order to live, they believe it will drop again. In fact if you look at leading historical indicators such as price to earnings ratios, stocks are still over-priced. If the market were to correct as much as it did during the Great Depression, the Dow would go to below 2,000! That's another 80% drop.

Further, many experts believe we haven't yet finished with the housing debacle; that we still have another go around of foreclosures. And we haven't even begun to consider what could happen when the credit card bubble bursts...and remember, bubbles always do burst eventually. That's why the call them bubbles.

Can you afford to take those bets? Maybe when you were younger. But now? I don't know. But I do know I would never recommend one of my clients take them. And none of my "Safe Harbor" clients...not one...has lost a dime in the market. Not ever. Don't believe me? Read on.

Perhaps it's time to start thinking differently about things. If so, maybe this book will help.

June 30, 2009

The Changing Tides

Nearly everything in life changes as you get older. Maybe you are a bit slower than you once were, or a bit more forgetful. On the other hand, maybe you aren't! Some people are healthier and sharper than they ever were. Either way, one thing is definitely true. Time is certainly more precious as you age, and you don't have as much time to make up for your mistakes. And that's why it is so important to understand the difference between accumulation and distribution.

Anyone who has a nest egg or retirement fund has some experience with accumulation. However, many believe that the same strategies used during the accumulation phase of their lives will also serve them well during the distribution phase of their lives.

Unfortunately, this is rarely the case, and your distribution "vessel" can literally be capsized by storms that would hardly have rocked your accumulation vessel.

Doubly unfortunate for retirees is that some planners and many brokers don't understand this; especially those who don't specialize in the needs of aging and retired people. Some will recommend their older clients use the same strategies they used when accumulating their wealth to distribute it. This can prove to be very poor advice. If you lost money during the recent meltdown, you have firsthand experience of this.

The first reason is very basic. During the accumulation phase of your life volatile markets can actually work to your benefit. This is managed through a technique called "dollar cost averaging." It works because as the price of shares goes down, you have the ability to purchase more shares for the same price. For example, if the price of a fund share is $35, and you are investing $175 per month in your retirement account, you can purchase five shares. But if the price goes down to $30 per share, that same $175 will purchase 5.83 shares. Now, since the overall trend in the market historically goes up over time, you have that additional .83 shares working for you to increase your wealth, for the entire time that you are accumulating your nest egg. So the volatility "storm" can be turned into a favorable wind that you can ride to greater wealth, *as long as you have enough time.*

When you are young and accumulating, time works in your favor because the overall trend in the market is historically upwards. However as you age the time you have to recover from a loss is much shorter. Time is now the enemy, so risk becomes much more dangerous than when you were young.

And, instead of accumulating, you are spending, or selling. Market volatility works just the opposite when you are in this distribution phase. Take a look at Figure 1, below.

Imagine you were on the red line (the market) and had to live on it during the years between 1999 and 2002 (perhaps this doesn't take so much imagination?!).

Every time you sell shares to live, you have to sell more than the period before...shares that are gone forever, and unavailable to you when the market recovers. It's the same as trying to sail a leaky boat!

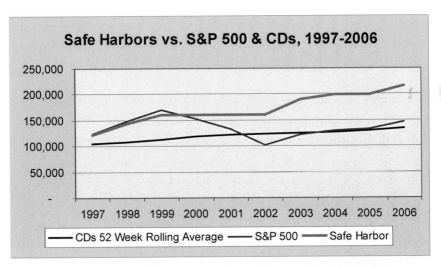

Figure 1: Safe Harbor performance 1997-2006 vs. S&P 500 and CDs

However, if you were on the green line (the Safe Harbor) your share value is protected during the down times, and available to help recover during the good. Now which line would you rather be on? Especially if you are spending?

Why do so many traditional planners and brokers not see these things? We don't know for sure, but we do have our theories.

Often when we ask people if they have a planner, they will say, "Sure…Smith Barney," or, "Edward Jones!"

Well, these are salesmen, pure and simple: not planners. Their job is to sell and trade stocks and securities…not financial planning.

Brokers can be great in the accumulation phase but are often found lacking during the retirement phase of life. And honestly, some aren't that good at anything besides selling and trading.

Let me be clear. My aim is not to attack your advisor. I am sure he or she has done a tremendous job helping you accumulate for retirement. I'm just saying, if you need to treat cancer, you don't go to a cardiologist...you go to an oncologist. Now that you are in the distribution phase of your life you may be better off with someone who specializes in distribution rather than accumulation.

Commissions and Fees

The truth is, Wall Street is not designed to help you distribute...it's designed to help you accumulate stocks and bonds. When you engage a stock broker, he or she makes his money by selling you securities, not by managing your money. Unless they are buying and selling, there is no money to be made. Remember that the next time you get a "hot tip." Here's a tip...your broker could be trying to make a trade so s/he can get a commission.

Other people use fee-based money managers. With a fee-based money manager, the fees are ongoing, every day, year after year. Whether you make money or lose it, you are paying fees. And often, taxes to boot.

You will find that I hit fees pretty hard in this book. I don't like them, and neither should you. They steal your money and don't really buy you anything...but more (and more!) about that later.

Look at how fees work to motivate your fee-based planner. Typically they charge between one to two percent of the amount of dollars...not shares...under management. In the past year, the market value of most securities has gone down a whopping 40%! What did that do to the fees your planner charges? Right...they went down 40%, too. Do you really think they are going to recommend that you take even more money away from them to make it safer? That's like taking the braces off their kids' teeth! Perhaps they more likely to urge you to "ride it out."

How long are you supposed to ride it out? And what about all those shares you have to sell to live while you're riding? Maybe you're just being taken for a ride?

"But things are getting better," you say. "Just look at how much the market has rebounded since the first of the year." Right. But just look at how fast it goes up and down these days. On October 19, 1987, a.k.a. "Black Monday," the Dow dropped over 508 points to lose 22.61% of its value. This is generally regarded as the worst day in trading history. However, today we hardly blink when the market loses or gains 500 points in a day. It just seems to be business as usual. Is this really what you want to bet your future on? Especially if you only have 10 or 15 years left?

Typically it takes years for markets to recover, and just hours for them to crash (that's why it's called a crash!). When you're older, that can spell doom for your retirement.

Fear And Greed: The Two Most Common Decision Factors in Driving Ordinary Investors

I recently met with a woman who had lost almost half of her money over the past 14 months (at the time of this writing, we have just weathered the worst downturn in history). She wanted to meet with me because she felt something was wrong (no kidding!!), but she was very afraid of making any changes. She had just lost almost $200,000 in the market (she had started with a little over $400,00).

And she is 71 and very worried (rightly so) about her future. *And all of her money is still in the market because her broker told her not to "lock in the losses...to just ride it out!"*

When I showed her we could move it into a safer place that could help her recover by locking in her gains each year, her response was, "Oh, I could never do that." When I asked her why, she said, "Because my broker has always been so nice to me!"

You would be amazed at how often I hear this. It almost seems like people would actually rather lose hundreds of thousands of dollars than offend a financial advisor they barely know!

But of course there is much more going on; even when people know their circumstances are terrible, just deciding to change can seem insurmountable. This is especially true as we get older, and it can work to our detriment if we are in a bad situation. So very often we fool ourselves into thinking the situation is not so bad after all...just so we won't have to change.

It's very strange. If you went to a mechanic and he broke your car, wouldn't you find another mechanic? If you went to a doctor and he made you sicker, wouldn't you find another doctor? If you hired a contractor to work on your house and he botched the job, wouldn't you hire another contractor?

So what's with this misplaced loyalty to financial advisors? Shouldn't your loyalty be to yourself? Here are some of the things I hear people say.

1. "But he did so well for me before this." Right! We were riding a bubble. Everything was going up, up, up. You could have made money in your sleep...without paying fees and charges! The true test of an advisor is how he or she does when the bubble bursts. How did yours do? If you lost 10-20 or even 50% of your wealth...I would submit, not so well.

2. "If I sell now, I lock in my losses." What's that mean? If the stocks you own were worth $100,000, and they are now worth $50,000, you've lost $50,000, whether you sell them or not. Your money is gone. Not "locking them in" only risks that you could lose some more. And if your advisor was so smart, why didn't he "lock in your earnings" when the market was up. Your boat is sinking. Get out of it while you still can, and get into a Safe Harbor that locks in your gains each year.

3. "My advisor is always so nice to me." Why wouldn't he be? He's gambling with your money. And just like the house, he'll make out whether you win or lose. Who wouldn't be nice to you?

4. "Everyone else has lost money, too." Even if that were true, so what? Are you a lemming following everyone else over the cliff? And the truth is, NOT everyone else has lost money. My clients haven't. Nor the clients of the other advisors on our team. Nor those of thousands of advisors all over the country who deal only in safe money. There are ways to profit handsomely without risking anything. And that's what this book is about.

5. "There is no way my advisor could have foreseen this." Poppycock! There is no way your advisor couldn't foresee this. You were in the MARKET. That's GAMBLING. And YOU ARE NO LONGER YOUNG. That means you have no time to recover when the market goes down. When it goes down it's normally very fast (why do you think it's called a crash?) and usually takes years to recover. And if your advisor doesn't know that, then s/he can't possibly keep you safe.

Take just a moment to look at the language of the market and it might clue you into how it works and how traders think. Think of the times when the market is good. How do news organizations describe the mood of these times? Words like "euphoric" come to mind, don't they? What about when times are bad? How about the word, "panic." Ever hear that one?

How about the term for a good market...a "bull market." Think of it. How does a bull behave? Are bulls intelligent? Or are they just thousands of pounds of raging muscle and bone charging at anything that moves?

What about the recent "bubbles" we've had. The "tech bubble," the "real estate bubble," and the "credit card bubble." And what happened to those bubbles? What happens to all bubbles? They "burst." And then the market "crashed."

Crash. Bubble. Euphoria. Panic. These are pretty graphic examples of the language of the market...and all of these are terms that are used commonly, every day the market is open. Are these the words you want to hang your economic future on?

Now, let's lift the hood a little higher. Let's talk about all the "experts" who "understand" the market and can tame this wild beast and bend it to their will and your advantage. You know...the "Masters of the Universe." The people who run firms like Lehman Brothers, Bear Stearns, Merrill Lynch, AIG, Wachovia Bank, Indy Mac, Washington Mutual, Wells Fargo... I think you're getting the picture. Here we had people who were making millions per year because they "understood" the market and guided it to...well, to the first and second crash of the 21st Century...all in the span of 10 short years!

What about the true gurus of the markets? The magicians who could make you rich. You know, the Bernie Madoffs of the world (I think he should write a book about his life. He could call it, "Madoff With Your Money.") Or Ken Lay, Michael Milken, Charles Keating, Ivan Boesky; and the list goes on and on. Are these the "experts" you want to hang your economic future on? Plenty of people did.

And the thing is, people just don't learn. I hear all the time from people that "the market will come back...it has to." Has to? Who says? The market sheriff? Your advisor? Your brother-in-law? Is that a "law" you want to hang your economic future on?

Let's think about it for a second...if the market went down 40% last year...and you lost 40% (which most people did), do you know how much it has to go up for you to just get back to even?

SIXTY-SEVEN PERCENT. That's right. Just to get back your 40% loss, the market has to go back up 67%. Is this a number you want to hang your economic future on?

Most people in the market have no idea what they are doing or why they are doing it. They rely on someone they don't really know to provide advice they have no way of judging the validity of, putting their entire livelihoods and futures into these near-strangers' hands. They ride a wave of fear and greed, euphoria when the market is up and panic when it's down, with no idea of who to turn to. And they take feeble comfort from such platitudes as "ride it out," "the market will rebound," "don't lock in your losses," and "everyone else lost money, too."

Consider this: there are more than 8,000 managed funds on the market, and over 80% of them lose to the indexes. *That means you have 6,400 chances out of 8,000 every time you pick a fund to lose your shirt.* Think about it...what are the odds that your advisor is going to steer you to the winning fund? What are the odds that he or she even represents the right companies? It's only one in five.

In fact, the average mutual fund investor after taking ALL the risk, makes less than 2%! The average advisor? 1.5%...*all on your money and risk!* Who wouldn't be "nice" to you?

We take a very different approach

Our job is different and very specific. Our job is to make sure that the money you have accumulated during your working years lasts and provides a comfortable retirement for the rest of your life; and then, after you die, to make sure it goes to your loved ones as quickly, efficiently—and with as few legal hassles and taxes—as possible. Without charging unnecessary fees or putting your hard-earned money at risk. A job we've been performing successfully for over four decades for thousands of clients.

Hazards That Can Swamp Your Ship and Sink Your Retirement

For purposes of this book we are using the ship metaphor for your estate. Your **estate** is everything you own. It's your real estate, your business, your rentals, and your money...your nest egg. Protecting that ship is what we mean when we say "Estate Planning."

Now that you are retired, or thinking about retiring, your estate...your ship...needs to take care of you. You may wish to have your ship sail you through a **comfortable retirement**, or you might want to pass it on to your **heirs** or a **charity**. Whatever it is, you don't want to have storms along the way sinking your "Ship of Estate." You want clear and smooth sailing.

Your vessel needs to be sound enough to take care of you both while you're alive and follow your wishes upon your demise. In other words, you want there to be no problems while you are living or after you are gone.

Now along the way there are several storms and other hazards that can swamp or even sink your ship and that should be of major concern to you. These are, in no particular order: fees, taxes, probate, creditors, inflation and risk. This book provides a "see-level" look at each of these hazards and provides some things you may be able to do about them, and that we have helped many others employ successfully.

The good news is that there are things you can do to shelter your estate from these hazards. "Safe Harbors," if you will. The further good news is that they really do work...nearly every time. We have been applying these principals for over 40 years, and we have seen them work successfully for thousands of clients. They may work for you, too.

Of course there are always special circumstances that can change the effectiveness and appropriateness of these solutions for each individual person. So it is very important that you don't act on any of these without speaking with a competent professional first.

You may have a planner that you think you are happy with, and you would never contemplate changing, and we aren't asking you to.

But the very fact that you are taking the time to read this book says you must have at least a vague feeling that things could be better. And usually they can.

So keep at it. You might just find the answers to the questions that are bothering you. We would be happy to consult with you about any questions you have, and there is never any charge for these consultations.

Oh, and one other thing...not a single one of our safe harbor clients has lost as much as a dime in this recent economic meltdown...or ever, for that matter. Not one.

If you are NOT in this category, perhaps you should get in touch right away...before your entire ship sinks and is gone forever. There ARE things that can be done.

The Tax Typhoon

Everyone is familiar with taxes. You have a silent partner in every transaction that you undertake. Most people can't even breathe without paying a tax!

The most common tax most people are familiar with is the **Income Tax.** You've probably been paying this tax all your life, on every dollar you earned. And guess what. Chances are you have been overpaying…and are still overpaying. Just getting this one area under control could give you substantially more money to work with. But most people don't even know where to begin.

Taxes can be insidious. For example, did you know you can end up paying taxes on mutual funds even when they lose money? Or that tax-free bonds can actually cost you more in taxes? It's true. It's covered in the "Safe Harbor From Taxes" section of this book.

And let's not even mention the 66% that many people pay on their qualified money! (Okay, we'll just mention it…66%, and sometimes more!). That's right, the government can take up to 66% *or more* of your IRA, 401(k), 403(b) or other qualified money! If you're slow on math, that leaves you and your heirs 34% of the savings you have worked your lifetime to accumulate!

In addition to the income tax there is the **Social Security Tax.** A lot of people are paying taxes on their Social Security benefits. You've paid a Social Security (payroll) tax all your working life and now it's time to collect on the promise.

So now Uncle Sam is paying you your Social Security benefit, but is taking up to 85% of that benefit (which you paid for) and counting it against you on your tax return. Does that seem right? And that Social Security tax is in addition to your regular income tax.

Another tax is the **Capital Gains Tax**. That has dropped down now and is 15% on a long-term capital gains. That seems really reasonable to some people. But the capital gains tax may end up being much higher. Why?

Beware the law of unintended consequences!

Because of the **Estate Tax**, which they are talking about repealing or dramatically reducing. You see, reducing or eliminating the estate tax means a significant loss of revenue that needs to be made up, especially with the trillions of dollars in debt we are carrying. So it currently appears that they will also most likely repeal *the fully stepped up valuation* on capital gains at death. It's already scheduled to expire in 2011, and it doesn't look like Congress is in the mood to reinstate it. If this happens, nearly every hard working family will be impacted – not just the rich! This represents billions of dollars in tax revenue.

There's another threat the estate tax repeal presents. The states share in a substantial amount of the revenue generated by the Federal Estate Tax. In most states, the estate and inheritance taxes are designed in such a way that states would face either a full or partial loss of revenues if the federal estate tax were repealed. In fact, approximately two-thirds of the states could face a total loss of estate tax revenue as a result of the federal repeal.

So where to find this lost revenue? You bet…increased State Inheritance Taxes! So, if the repeal of the Federal Estate tax goes through, you are facing the loss of the step up in value on your capital gains, and you could end up paying every bit as much in state inheritance taxes. What a country!

Double Jeopardy

The chart below shows how damaging true cost of taxes can be. This shows the comparison between a traditional investment... CDs, and one of the key Safe Harbor strategies we discuss later in this book. This chart tracks a $250,000 initial investment over a 15 year period of time at a 15% tax rate. Note how these modest tax rates can steal so much of potential growth and recovery?

Why is it so much? And why does a total tax bill of $62,470 (in the taxes column) cost nearly three times more in the "Total Cost of Taxes" column?

Because if you paid the taxes to Uncle Sam, you don't have that money to accrue over time in interest! And the lost opportunity cost is much more that just the initial taxes paid. That's a "one-two punch"!

In this case, the taxable, "safe" strategy, costs over $150,000 more than a Safe Harbor "Income for Life" plan such as those our clients might use.

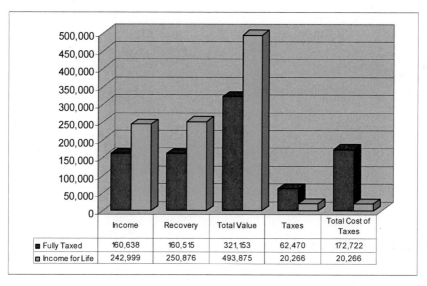

	Income	Recovery	Total Value	Taxes	Total Cost of Taxes
■ Fully Taxed	160,638	160,515	321,153	62,470	172,722
▢ Income for Life	242,999	250,876	493,875	20,266	20,266

Figure 2: Effect of taxes on a $250,000 investment over 15 years, accounting for taxes paid, and the opportunity cost of the taxes.

The Probate Squall

The next storm waiting to swamp your boat is **Probate**. Probate is a storm that can be very rough on the Ship of Estate. And, what most people don't understand is that probate can negatively impact you while you're still alive, just as significantly as after you are gone. This can happen if you become incapacitated and are unable to manage your affairs. If you do not have the right documents in place, the probate court will step in and take over for you.

What is probate? Simple…it's the distribution of your probative property once you are dead or incapacitated. What's that? It's any property that is not jointly owned (like a house or checking account) or contractually promised (like a life insurance policy or annuity with a beneficiary). Further, many people believe that if they have a will, they won't have to go through probate. That's entirely wrong…in fact it's your will that directs the probate.

The main problem with probate is that the average delay nationwide is about **one to three years.** In other words, your estate could be frozen for the period of time that probate proceedings and the validating of your will and the retitling of your assets happen.

Here's an example. A few years ago my wife's grandmother died leaving behind an estate worth about $400,000. She was quite old; in her 90's. She lived in a nursing home, her house had been sold, and all she left behind were a few personal items plus about $400,000 in cash and liquid assets.

She wanted each of her grandchildren to get a portion of her estate. My wife's was about $18,000, which came in really handy...when we finally got it. You see, it took over a year for her very simple estate to go through probate!

Unfortunately, during this time the lawyers were getting their fees. So do you think that it is in the best interest of the legal profession to wrap up this process quickly? Could that be why probate is dragged out over such a long and tedious time frame?

Further, if you own property in more than one state you could be exposed to more than one probate process.

Our opinion...and that of some lawyers we know, is that probate exists primarily for the enrichment of the legal profession. That's important to understand....the lawyers make money off your estate. One lawyer friend of mine calls probate his ARP (Attorney Retirement Plan).

So why don't they change it? Well 83% of the politicians are current or former attorneys. So don't expect probate to go away. It's a cash cow for the profession!

Another unsavory aspect of probate is that it is a matter of **public record.** Anyone can pull your public probate records and snoop through your affairs. If you're okay with that, well fine. But do you really want any neighbor, acquaintance, creditor, etc., to know what you had and where it went? Public records can cause other problems, too. Unscrupulous fake "creditors" can make claims against your estate and your estate and executor could be forced to settle or deal with them. This can increase the delay and the legal fees; not to mention the money lost in settlement.

By avoiding probate you can keep your affairs private and your assets safe! And it's really easy and inexpensive to do. But you have to plan, and you have to plan while you are still alive!

Solutions to probate are covered later in this book.

The Creditor Feeding Frenzy

A creditor is any party that lays claim to the assets held by another. This can happen at any time...even if you don't owe any money. Further, this is potentially the worst threat, because it can totally wipe out your estate like a giant swarm of sharks .

It can come from anywhere. One that many seniors have to deal with is the **nursing home**. Have you ever known someone who has lost their entire estate to a nursing home? I have.

This is called *Estate Recovery*. If you go to a nursing home, a lien will be recorded against your house. In fact, against any property you own in your name. You may have heard that if you go to the nursing home, you can have one car, a house, and $2,000. That's true, but only until you're dead. That's when the nursing home will exercise its lien, and then the heirs can lose the family homestead. This can be devastating. And it's easily avoided.

Another common creditor is a **lawsuit**. A lawsuit can come from any source. One in three Americans gets sued every year. Currently in America there are almost 1,000,000 attorneys. Every year more than 100,000 more lawyers come out of law school. There aren't enough good cases! They need to eat...and just like sharks they feed off anything swimming nearby. Why not you?

Do you own rental property? If you do, you need to understand that chances are you will be sued. Statistically, business owners and landlords get sued more than any other group. If you're sued you better not own that property in your name! Here's an important concept—ownership should be separated from control. Control is good; ownership is bad. Why? Because if you own it, it can be taken from you.

Some people think they can avoid probate (and other issues, such as nursing home expenses) by putting their assets in their children's names. I can't tell you how many times people have told me their house is in their kids' names...or they are on the deed...or the checking account...or other assets.

In my opinion, this is a TERRIBLE way to go, because the main result is your jointly-held property is subject to law suits, divorces, bankruptcies, creditors and who knows what else...not only against you, but *against your children as well*.

What if, for example, your daughter had friends of her children playing at her house? And when she wasn't looking, those kids all got on their bikes and rode out into the street.

Bang...the friend is hit by a car and has major medical bills. Who are his parents going after? Do you think maybe that house of yours is a target? Well you better believe it will be on their list. To their attorney, you are just a big fat meal ticket, and when people are desperate, they will do nearly anything.

Or say your daughter gets divorced and her ne'r-do-well husband starts going after her assets? Guess whose house is on his list? Once sharks start to feed, nothing is safe!

So we don't want to start giving away assets while we are still alive...but we do want them protected in case of death or debilitating disease or accidents.

You don't have to *lose* a lawsuit to have everything in your estate frozen. A lawsuit can freeze some – or most likely all – of your estate even prior to the legal proceedings and prior to a judgment. A simple Writ of Attachment can cause you to lose control of all your assets for years while the court is figuring out who wins. But when lawyers are involved, we know who loses, right?

The Inflation Thunder Storm

The next hazard is **inflation**. Inflation has been pretty much kept in check lately, but keep in mind that inflation has to happen. We depend on it.

Inflation helps drive our economy. Lately there has been talk of "deflation," or the ongoing reduction in prices. That's what happened to Japan in the 1990s that caused all the pain there. Why are lower prices bad? That sounds like a good thing. Well, if you think the price of something is going down, you are more apt to wait a while before you buy it. So people get out of the habit of buying things. Less and less money is spent, and the economy tends to spiral downward. This can lead to depression.

Another reason that we depend on inflation is because we are carrying huge amounts of debt...both national and personal. There are only three ways to handle a deficit...revenue, repudiation, and inflation.

First is revenue. For the government that means taxes. But it really can't levy taxes up to or beyond the ability to repay the deficit, because it would be political suicide. We have huge tax rates already. Raising taxes is not the best answer to dealing with our deficit. And neither the Congress nor the Administration seem to have the appetite to raise them. In fact, lowering taxes seems to be the mantra of the day.

The second way to deal with the debt and deficits is repudiation.

As soon as we do that and we renege on our debts worldwide, our economy collapses. It's like the devaluing of the ruble in Russia a few years ago. Once the confidence is lost because we are no longer able to repay or we will no longer honor our debts as a nation, our dollar and our economy are no longer any good. So that's really not a good solution to deficits.

The third and perhaps the most viable way to handle deficits is through inflation. *Inflation allows us to repay current debts with discounted dollars in the future.* Our society has a vested interest in keeping inflation alive and healthy, so don't expect inflation to go away and don't expect deflation really to happen anytime too soon. The powers that be can't afford to let that happen.

Now inflation has traditionally run about 2.7% annually. Most cost of living adjustments are along the order of 3%. So if your assets are earning around 3% per year (or even 4-5%, taxed), what's happening? That inflation threat is slowly swamping your Ship of Estate and it's hurting your ability to live off of it. Further... it might even die before you do, which puts you in a world of real hurt. <u>You don't want your estate to die before you do</u>.

And, after you're gone and your estate goes to your heirs, why would you let it continue to shrink?

So the rule of thumb, or at least our rule of thumb, is a minimum return of **6%**. You want to make sure your estate is growing at least at 6%. The reason 6% is so important is because it's double the traditional rate of inflation.

Further, you want that 6% to be after tax or at least, tax deferred, or it does you very little good.

However, if the rate of inflation rises, you want the rate of return to rise, too. So it's very important to have your money in something that can go up with the rate of inflation. How to do this is exactly what this book is about.

Did you know that with a Writ, a creditor can go right into your bank account and drain your funds? It doesn't matter what your circumstances are. It's true.

You have to take definite steps to deal with the creditor hazard., but you don't ever want to give another party control over your estate.

In my opinion the creditor hazard is by far the worst threat because it can completely wipe out your estate.

Compare creditors to taxes. Your estate can usually survive taxes…there may be less at the end, but there is usually *something*. It will be pummeled but it can survive. Probate is the same way. Your estate may be frozen for a period of time and might have to pay some fees and taxes, but in the end the estate is still there.

Lawsuits and nursing homes, however, can wipe out *everything*.

There are a couple of really easy and inexpensive ways to mitigate the threat of lawsuits. The first is insurance. Most homeowners' policies are capped at about $250,000 in liability protection, so they seldom will adequately protect you if you are sued.

However, by purchasing an umbrella liability policy you can protect yourself against lawsuits. These are really inexpensive…about $200-$300 per year for $1 million in coverage. You get them through the company that provides your homeowners' policy, and they can bind you right on the phone. This is one of the least expensive ways to protect your assets if you are sued.

Secondly, you want to make sure your valuable assets are not in your name…or the names of your relatives. They must be put in trust, which is covered later in the book.

Nursing homes, too, can deplete everything you have. The average cost of care is over $100,000 per year, and one out of two people will need care before they die. Statistically that means if you are married, you and your spouse have a 100% chance one of you will require care.

So it is very important to do some planning for the nursing home iceberg. That is also covered later in the book.

Risk Can Sink Your Ship

We all know risk can cause you to lose **money**. But the important thing to remember for retirees is that risk is NOT about losing money. IT IS ABOUT LOSING TIME. You can get the money back with enough time. But you cannot get the time back, and that's why you must eliminate risk as you get older. You are no longer in the accumulation phase of your life; you are in the deaccumulation, or spending phase.

> **"Rule #1, don't lose your money; Rule #2, see rule #1"**
> **- Warren Buffett**

Anyone who is approaching or past age 60 shouldn't care as much about <u>accumulation</u> strategies as they care about <u>preservation</u> and <u>distribution</u> strategies. At these ages if you expose your estate to risk, you could end up losing it. What good does it do you to gain 20% or 30% in a given year only to give it all back, and then some, in the following year? Even if it comes back, how much time have you lost crawling out of that hole?

Anyone who's facing retirement now should be well aware of this. We have gone through two major market corrections in the past decade. First in 2000 and 2001 as the market corrected for the tech bubble. And now more recently in the past 18 months as it corrected again. These times have been very painful for people.

Figure 3 on the following page illustrates the problem very well. It shows a 10 year period where the gains in the market averaged

Figure 3: Impact of losses on income stream

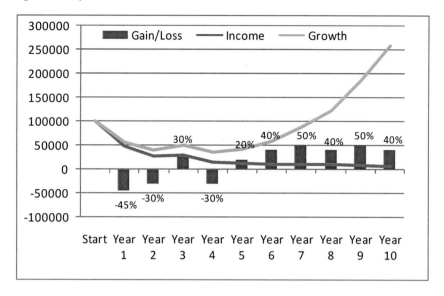

10% (the green line). Without taking withdrawals, that $100,000 grows to $259,000. So, now lets see what happens if we take just $6000 a year in income for 10 years...the blue line.

Amazingly, even though the average return over this 10 year period is 10%, and the amount earned is $159,000, it all changes as soon as you begin to take income (even a modest amount). The reason, of course, is that taking income in the down years removes funds that are necessary to the recovery.

Bottom line: taking money out of a volatile account tends to magnify losses. Non existent shares can't appreciate. The damage is done, and compounded, over and over again. You simply cannot afford to utilize such an account for income purposes if you want to guarantee that you won't run out of money.

How to avoid this scenario? Carve off a fixed income account that generates income whether the market is up or down. Then you can "swing for the fences" with your growth account without having to worry about risk causing you to run out of money. This is covered extensively in the Safe Harbors section later in this book.

Here's another reason that time is so critical when talking about risk. It takes two to three times longer to regain market losses than it did to accumulate the money in the first place (say what?).

Here's what I mean. Assume you have, over the past 10 years, accumulated $100,000 in the stock market. Then last year hit, and you followed your advisor's advice and just "rode it out." Now you're down 40% to $60,000.

It's okay, though, because your advisor has assured you that the market will rebound and everything will be just fine. All you have to do is wait for the market to go back up 40% and everything will be fine...right?

Not so much. In fact, if the market rebounds 40% you will only recover just over half your losses! Want proof? Okay:

$$60,000 \times 1.40 = 84,000$$

In fact, the market would have to go up 67% just for you to get back to square one. Now, how long do you think it will take for the market to rebound 67%?

The average time, during the 20th Century, for the market to rebound after a significant correction was 17 years! Seventeen years to get back to even. Do you even have 17 years left? Do you want to stake your financial future on it?

Here are some examples: In 1929 after the crash, it took 24 years for people to get back to even. In 1966, it took 16 years. In 1990, though the Dow rode the tech bubble up, the Nikkei index took over 17 years to recover, and the NASDAQ hasn't come close to recovering yet. In fact it's still at less than one half of its high.

Zero Is Your Hero

So knowing all this, how do you turn it to your advantage? That's where we come in with our Safe Harbor strategies. You see, our Safe Harbor strategies will pay you a portion of the market gains when the market goes up, but preserve your principal and lock in your gains when the market is down.

Imagine how much money you could make if you never lost any! Imagine if every time the market goes up over a period of time, you could enjoy a significant portion of those gains, without every having to worry about market losses. What if you had an advisor who could so accurately time the market (he/she doesn't exist!), that he could buy and sell your stocks at exactly the right time to avoid losses but realize gains? Wouldn't you run to him or her? Even if they took, say, half the profits they made for you? Why wouldn't you? What could you possibly have to lose?

Essentially, that's what Safe Harbor strategies do. They guarantee you will never lose a penny of your principal or accrued interest. And they give you a portion of market gains, without ever losing to the market. So you are always either staying even, or going up. So if the market goes up a little, you could make a little. If it goes up a lot, you could make a lot. But if it goes down? How much do you lose? Right. Zero. Zero is your hero! Here's a graph comparing the S&P 500 (red line) over the past 10 years with a typical fixed indexed annuity (Safe Harbor) strategy (blue line):

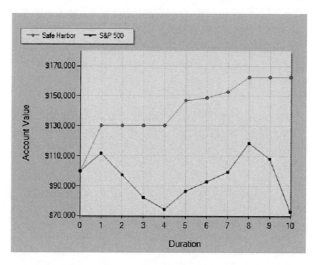

Figure 4: Demonstrates how simply eliminating losses from your portfolio can impact long-term growth and maximize financial security.

Fees: Pirates of Your Future

Like taxes, fees are a bandit that can steal your future. People often don't realize how much fees cost them. The truth is they are a pirate that can literally board and sink your ship.

Assume your money is under management with a financial professional who is charging you the average rate of 1%-2% to manage your money (1.66% is the national average). What does that translate to in real dollars?

Say you are 70 years old and have $600,000 that you want to

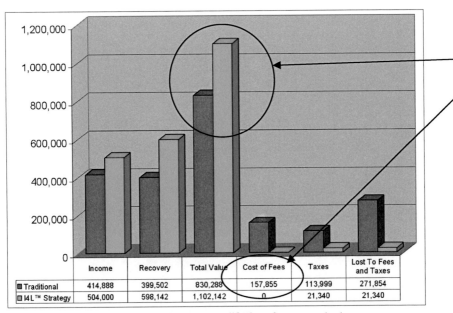

	Income	Recovery	Total Value	Cost of Fees	Taxes	Lost To Fees and Taxes
Traditional	414,888	399,502	830,288	157,855	113,999	271,854
I4L™ Strategy	504,000	598,142	1,102,142	0	21,340	21,340

Figure 5: Impact of fees and taxes on a lifetime income strategy

move into a secure income strategy. Your broker, who has done a decent job (we think we can do better) in building up that $600,000 during your accumulation phase, has rightly moved your money into less risky strategies, and your overall return is reduced to 5%-6%. But that's okay because you understand the difference between accumulation and distribution and don't want to lose money if (when) the market declines again.

However, since you are paying 1.5% in fees (approximate national average), you are really only receiving 3.5% - 4.5% in return. That's a reduction of between 25% and 30% of your income! That means that you may have to substantially reduce your income, or settle for less, later.

Fees also incur an interest cost based on the amount of money unavailable to earn interest that went to fees. So each year the cost of fees is magnified by the earnings lost to previously paid fees. Figure 5, on the previous page, provides an illustration of the total difference in between a fee-based model and a Safe Harbor Account without fees, presuming beginning average rate of return of 6% for both over 15 years. Notice how the cumulative total loss to fees over 15 years is $157,855, just for letting your advisor hold your money in low-risk , low-return strategies.

But those are just the fees that your money manager charges. They are nothing compared to what the financial industry takes. The worst culprit of all are mutual funds, and they are covered next.

Hidden Dangers of Mutual Funds

Many people believe that investing for the long term in a diversified portfolio of mutual funds is the smart thing to do. Let's check that out.

Setting risk aside just for a moment, one of the main problems with funds is again those pesky fees. Unlike other investments, the longer you invest in a mutual fund, the more you pay in fees. When you buy a piece of real estate or make a stock trade, you pay a commission. Once. But when you purchase a mutual fund, you pay a sales commission for as long as you own the fund!

That's why the return on investment is much lower on mutual funds — and why gains get lower the longer you own them. Could it be the reason most financial planners and financial companies recommend you invest for the long term is because the longer you hold on to the fund, the more money they make? Nah!

Just how much does a fund company make from investors who hang in there for the long term?

John Bogle, the founder of the Vanguard Group, addressed this when asked by a TV interviewer for the PBS show, *Frontline*, "What percentage of growth is going to fees in a 401(k) plan?"

Bogle replied, "Well it's awesome...an individual who's 20 years old today is starting to accumulate for retirement.... That person has about 45 years to go before retirement — 20 to 65 — and then, if you believe the actuarial tables, another 20 years to go before death.... So that's 65 years of investing. If you invest $1,000 at the beginning of that time and earn 8 percent, that $1,000 will grow...to around $140,000."

"Now the financial system — the mutual-fund system in this case — will take about 2.5 percentage points out of that return, so you'll have a net return of 5.5 percent, and your $1,000 will grow to approximately $30,000 to you the investor."

(Editors Note: In case you're wondering...we've done the math, and John Bogle is 100% correct.)

Bogle continued: "Think about that. That means the financial system put up zero percent of the capital and took zero percent of the risk and got almost 80 percent of the return. And you, the investor in this long time period, an investment lifetime, put up 100 percent of the capital, took 100 percent of the risk, and got only a little bit over 20 percent of the return."

Here's how that might look on a chart:

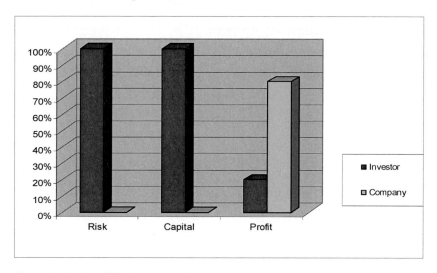

Figure 6: A simplified picture of how the return is split over the long term — and who takes the risk. Remember...you are (in) the red! You put up all the risk and all the capital and receive only 20% of the profits. Think there's a reason Wall Street wants you to invest for the long term? Aren't you ready for a better way?

Mutual Fund Taxes—Rubbing Salt in the Wounds

One of the most vexing areas of taxation is the way mutual funds are taxed. And by far the most troubling question of all is,

Do I really have to pay taxes on mutual funds even when they lose money and I don't take any income from them? And WHY?

First it's important to understand what mutual funds are. Large groups of investors pool their resources together to purchase positions in a mix of several or many different securities that are owned by the fund. This is done to try to make them perform in a certain way; safety, growth, income generation, etc. The fund manager will buy and sell different securities at different times to try to achieve the fund's stated goals. Presumably, the fund manager will buy low and sell high, thereby generating growth and profits for the investors.

However, we all know this doesn't always work (in fact it works way less than most people think: an ugly truth the industry doesn't want you to know is that the average equity investor has earned just 2.7% per year since 1984.*

By law, mutual funds must declare distributions each year. These distributions represent a profit the fund made when buying and selling securities. This is true even if you elect to leave it in the fund as reinvested dividends are considered taxable payments.

Even in years with negative returns, mutual funds can, and must, pay out distributions. Gains are calculated by taking the price the fund sold an individual security for and subtracting the purchase price (cost basis). It doesn't matter if the securities that the fund held were doing poorly, all that matters is that the fund sold the security at a profit and must now pay out the profits in the form of a distribution, which is a taxable event for the shareholder (you).

*Bogle, John C., "The Emperor's New Mutual Funds," *Bogle Financial Markets Research Center*, July 8, 2003

To better understand how this could happen, imagine your fund bought a security five years ago for $12 a share. At the start of this year the security was worth a total of $30 a share, but the fund ended up selling the security for only $25 a share. This is a loss for the year, but an overall profit of $13 a share. So even though the value of your fund went down, the profit on that individual security is taxed!

Another possibility would be for the fund to sell the security for $30 a share, which is a gain even for the most current year, but the bulk of the fund's holdings went down and created a losing year for the fund. This fund would still be forced to pay out capital gains on the securities that they sold for a profit...even though the value of the fund dropped.

This is exacerbated by the fact that most funds hold most securities less than 12 months. Therefore taxes are assessed at the higher short term capital gain rate, rather than the long term rate.

Adding Insult to Injury

Let's look at that again. In some years, funds with losses wind up selling winners to lock in cash balances, with the result of having a large tax bill on top of a losing year. And often, in order to avoid massive loss of confidence, managers will sell their best winners to shore up a losing fund. Therefore you can actually end up being taxed the most when your fund performs the worst!

Many people are unaware of the problem because profits (losses!) and taxes are separated. They get a year-end statement showing a loss or profit. A few weeks later they get a 1099-DIV form in the mail, and pass it along to their tax preparer, and they have forgotten about the statement.

One recent study found that 44% of the typical stock fund's performance from 1970 to 1995 was destroyed by federal taxes!*

*"Taxing Mutual Funds," *Ask SmartMoney: Personal Finance*

How Safe Are Your CDs?

Many people believe that CDs offer the best safety. Chances are you have or had a CD, or Certificate of Deposit. CDs often make up a sizeable portion of people's assets. Most people consider them to be a very Safe Harbor. Let's take a look.

First, do you **pay taxes** on a CD? Sure you do. You pay income tax on the interest, and that interest may also result in an increase in the percentage of Social Security earnings subject to income tax. Interest from CDs can also drive up your tax bracket. So CDs, right off the bat, are vulnerable to the tax storm.

Now, what about **probate**? Will your CD be subject to probate? Chances are it will because it is considered an asset that would need to be frozen until the will is validated and title is transferred. So a CD may be tied up for years in probate.

If a **lawsuit** occurs can they attach your CD? Sure. If you go to the **nursing home** is your CD exempt from counting as an asset? Well, yes. So it's very vulnerable to many types of creditors and other factors outside of your control.

Now let's look at **inflation**. Is your CD keeping up with inflation? Probably not. It's probably shrinking. By the time you get 2%-3% on your CD and pay a portion of that in tax, you are probably getting something less than the inflation rate.

So is a CD really a Safe Harbor? Well from the perspective of **market risk**, maybe so. But, if you view all of these other factors as risk to your nest egg, then it turns out CDs can be a safety concern after all, and may not do the job.

So when considered more carefully, it turns out that a very popular "Safe Money" savings plan may not be so safe after all!

Safe Harbors That Protect Your Retirement and Preserve Your Estate

When we speak of **Safe Harbors** we are really talking about **sheltering** your estate from these dangers, while providing you a comfortable and reliable income. We want to get your "ship of estate" out of harm's way and park it in a safe harbor. We want to **reposition** it. So the sheltering of the estate is probably the most important step and it's a simple maneuver. And as soon as we do that, we take it out of the danger zone. It is resting in safe harbors. Now what are some of those safe harbors, or tools that we use, and how can they help you?

This section will outline just some of those tools and give an example or two of how each can help. It is not designed to provide a complete strategy for all situations.

And it's important to remember that each individual will have their own special set of circumstances that may modify or influence the principals used here, so it is imperative that you seek advice from a professional before implementing these plans.

Leave a Paper Trail

Legal documents encompass anything from a basic will and medical power of attorney to a complex family trust. Legal documentation constitutes the basic estate planning tool, and without it you are completely exposed to anything life (or death) can throw at you.

In the context of the our deadly storms, the legal documentation provides the sound vessel, or foundation, for everything else we do. It determines what happens to you if you become incapacitated or die, and makes sure YOUR wishes are carried out! Yet, despite the importance of legal documentation in an estate plan, it is estimated that seven out of ten Americans die without a valid will and have no durable power of attorney.

Just how important is this? Do you remember Terri Schiavo? While that was an extreme case that captured much media attention, it was not out of the ordinary. In fact, if you were to become incapacitated right now, it could happen to you. A family decimated all because you didn't take an hour out of your life to put down in writing what you'd want to happen to you if you were disabled and couldn't speak for yourself.

A Financial Blueprint of Your Assets

A will is an instrument you can use to distribute your probate assets to your loved ones after you are gone. (Probate assets generally refer to those assets in your name only that do not pass to another at your death by contract or beneficiary designation.) Think of your will as the financial blueprint of your probate assets. Your will clearly states who will inherit those assets.

At death, the court rules on the validity of your will. If the will is valid, the court instructs your executor to carry out the terms of the will according to your wishes. (This act is known as an order of probate.) The executor is the person appointed by you in the will to supervise the distribution of your probate assets.

What Are the Consequences of Not Having a Will?

Without a will, you increase the likelihood of conflicts, bitterness, and after-death disputes between your children and other family members. *Here's how*: If you die without a valid will, the court does not have your blueprint to follow. Therefore, it has no way of knowing how to distribute your assets.

By "dying intestate," you lose the ability to direct the distribution of your estate. The state where you lived steps in at your death and makes the decisions for you, according to the distribution schedule set forth in its probate laws. The state's decisions are designed to pass property to those they think would most benefit. Unfortunately, the state's decisions may not conform to your wishes or to what is best for the people closest to you. This can cause a multitude of problems and misunderstandings, not to mention tying up your assets in the probate process for years.

Here's a true story about my Mother. Her Mom and Dad got divorced when she was a young woman. Now my Mom is 80 years old, and divorce in those days was rather rare, but it did happen, and it happened in my Mom's family.

Well the years went by and after a while my Grandfather married my "Grandmother Martha," whom I met once or twice when I was a child. Grandfather died when I was quite young, and it was a very difficult time for my Mom. She hadn't had that much contact with him in recent years, and had always missed that special time she remembered having with her father. At the time of his death, most of his wealth went to "Grandmother Martha," and nobody really thought about it until years later, when she died.

And that's when we found out that neither my Mom nor her sister got a thing to remember my Grandfather by. It had all gone to my step grandmother, and she left everything to her kids. Mom and my aunt didn't get a memento. They didn't get a remembrance of any kind. And they certainly didn't get a dime of his considerable wealth. Every bit of it went to "Grandmother Martha's" kids by her previous husband. People who were total strangers to my family, and really mere acquaintances to my grandfather. This was very painful for both my Mom and my aunt.

Now I am sure these are fine and deserving people. And they certainly were entitled to whatever belonged to their mother. But is it really right that my grandfather's entire lineage was cut out of not only his wealth, but also every remnant of his personal life? Is that what he really would have wanted? Is that what you'd want for your children and grandchildren? I don't believe it is.

So if a will is such an important document, why don't more people have one? Unfortunately, creating a will forces you to come face to face with your own mortality—and dealing with death is difficult for most people.

But, it will be much more difficult for your loved ones after you are gone if you don't prepare a will. And you will feel so much better when you have it done.

Common Misconceptions

Here are some of the more common rationalizations for not creating a will, and the facts that dispel those "myths."

Myth: "My assets are so small that a will is not necessary."

Fact: Few people are worth so little that a will is not necessary. Add together the value of your home, car, furniture, jewelry, savings account, and investment portfolio. Subtract from this total your personal debts. Most people are worth more than they think. Even if some items do not hold great monetary value, they could hold an enormous amount of sentimental value. Failing to indicate who receives these family treasures in your will can cause friction between family members that lasts for decades. Many families never recover.

Myth: "When I die, my spouse will get all of my assets."

Fact: If you and your spouse own assets jointly, at death your share of the assets will automatically go to the surviving spouse. However, if they are not jointly owned they will be split between your spouse and your children according to whatever state you reside in. And what happens when your spouse dies? What will your children receive? Does your spouse have the financial know-how to manage the family wealth? If your spouse remarries, some or all of your spouse's assets may wind up in the hands of his/her new spouse. Remember my Grandfather.

Myth: "I can create a will on my own and save the legal costs."

Fact: "Do-it-yourself" wills are frequently incomplete and ruled invalid by the courts. A vaguely-worded clause can result in lengthy legal battles. Anyone who might benefit from the invalidation of your will can contest it, and if the courts decide in his or her favor your estate may be required to cover all legal costs. Remember, the few dollars you save now could cost your loved ones thousands of dollars and much grief later.

Myth: "I don't want my final wishes to be set in stone. I'll create a will later in my life."

Fact: A will is an extremely flexible document whose terms can be changed as often as needed. In fact, any legal expert will tell you that a will should be re-examined periodically to make sure it is up to date. A will should receive a checkup whenever there is a substantial change in your life. Remember, the terms of a will only become effective at death.

Speaking From Beyond the Grave

A trust is a legal entity that holds assets for the benefit of another. Basically, it's like a container that holds money or property for somebody else.

You create a trust by executing a legal document called a trust agreement. The trust agreement names the beneficiaries and trustee(s), and contains instructions about what benefits the beneficiaries will receive, what the trustee's duties are, and when the trust will end, among other things.

How can a trust help?

We can use a trust for many purposes, for example, to avoid paying capital gains or estate taxes or to immediately stop probate. A family trust has many advantages, not the least of which is making sure your wishes are followed – exactly.

We call it "speaking from beyond the grave."

My Grandfather, for example, could have set up a trust that took care of Grandmother Martha for as long as she lived (clearly his intent), but that also made sure that anything left over was divided so that his children and grandchildren would benefit as well as his stepchildren.

Or you could leave your assets to a trust to take care of a special needs child, or grandchild. Or to pay for college educations. Or to delay payment of a gift until you are sure your children or grandkids are ready. Or to protect it from a spendthrift child (or spouse of one). Or many other things.

Here are some other examples of the power of a trust:

- It can eliminate probate and help with estate taxes, as long as it's set up properly.

- It gives you total control.

- It is private.

How can you know if you should learn more about a trust? Ask these four simple questions:

1) Do you own any real estate in your name?

2) Is your property, when added up, worth more than $100,000?

3) Do you have any children under the age of 18 who might inherit property from you?

4) Do you have any special needs children or grandchildren?

If the answer to any of them is yes, then a trust might be very beneficial to you.

Funding a trust

You can put almost any kind of asset in a trust, including cash, stocks, bonds, insurance policies, real estate, and artwork. The assets you choose to put in a trust will depend largely on your goals.

For example, if you want the trust to generate income, you should put income-producing assets, such as bonds, in your trust. Or, if you want your trust to create a fund that can be used to pay estate taxes or provide for your family at your death, you might fund the trust with a life insurance policy.

There are many types of trusts, the most basic being revocable and irrevocable. The type of trust you should use will depend on what you're trying to accomplish.

Clearly, trusts can be very useful, but not every trust is a fit for everybody, so you need to talk to an expert.

Spread Your Risk

Consider my friend, John, who I met soon after I got into this business. At the time, John was 48 years old and lived with his wife Sarah and their three young kids, Owen - eleven, Jeff- seven, and Jessie, who is three. Five years earlier, when he was 43, John was diagnosed with cancer and had to have major surgery.

I learned of his situation one day soon after I met John. We were sitting in our backyard watching our kids swim, and we got to talking about our jobs. I shared with John my reluctance about approaching friends about buying life insurance; that I always felt like my friends would think I was "on the make."

At that point John became very quiet. Then he told me about his cancer and that at the time of his diagnosis the only life insurance he had was a $50,000 term life policy through his work. And now he can't get any more.

John told me about how he constantly worries about what would happen to his kids if the worst were to happen; about how they would get through college. He told me the biggest regret in his whole life was that he didn't provide for his family while he still could. He told me he wished someone like me had made him sit down and listen, and that I should never be shy about sharing what I know with people.

My heart breaks for John. He's a good man. He works hard and loves his family dearly. He's one of the finest people I know. He worries constantly about what will happen to his family. And I can't help him. That was a valuable lesson for me. I have never been bashful since.

100% of us are going to die. Yet over 40% of us don't have any life insurance at all. And of those who do, it's estimated that over 50% are under-insured. It's one of the most important things you can do for your family. And one of the most neglected.

Torpedo Your "Death Taxes"

Many people believe that if they have lots of assets they don't need life insurance. Nothing could be further from the truth. In fact, the more assets you have, the more insurance you need.

Malcolm Forbes, who had $40 million in life insurance when he died, was reported to have said that if he'd known what a great bargain it was, he would have had twice that amount!

Estate and inheritance taxes are a fact of life that can have the effect of a tidal wave against your estate.

Further, if you have qualified money (IRA, 401(k), or another qualified pension plan), it is likely to be taxed more than once. First, there is the IRD tax (Income Tax in Respect to the Decedent), a fancy way of saying that if you don't pay taxes on it now, your heirs will after you die. Then there is any estate and inheritance tax due.

Any way you look at it, death taxes can be a nightmare for your heirs. And it's lots worse if you have an estate that is top heavy in things like stocks or real estate, because your loved ones could be forced to sell at fire sale prices in order to pay the taxes.

This is a problem we frequently run into. Some people try to deal with it through gifting (either directly to their heirs, or by setting up a charitable trust or foundation). And often that's appropriate.

But even more often, the best answer is also the simplest: life insurance. Life insurance is the only financial instrument there is that can instantaneously create a pool of tax-free cash, outside of your estate, at the exact time when your heirs need it the most.

Simply put, there is no other "investment" that can possibly pay off as well. Assuming you are 65 a year old male rated standard, you would have to earn the following returns if you collected on a tax-free life policy at the following ages:

Age at Death	Comparable IRR
70	109.49%
75	31.05%
80	15.76%
85	9.93%
90	7.42%
95	5.48%

All with no risk to principal, no fees, and no taxes. And perhaps most important of all is the emotional relief it provides. During a time of great loss, you have saved your loved ones from going through financial strife as well. Could there really be a more genuine display of love and compassion?

Here's a great example of how we recently helped one major client...call him Bob.

Bob is very top heavy in real estate...about $15 million. Having already gifted about $10 million to his heirs, he has already maxed out his giving. And with the recent bath real estate has taken, he has very little cash to his name.

Bob is faced with a huge inheritance tax bill should he die any time soon: approximately half his estate. And with the real estate markets as depressed as they currently are, he knows his estate would be in very bad shape should his heirs be forced to sell off properties to pay taxes.

We calculated that his heirs would need to generate about $8 million to cover his estate taxes. With the market in its current state, Bob believes that means they would have to liquidate at least $10 million, and perhaps $12 million in order to cover the tax bill. And Uncle Sam only gives you nine months to do it, unless you borrow and pay interest. This could literally devastate his estate.

Bob thought this problem was insurmountable. He knew he was in a desperate situation, but the last quote for life insurance he received that would be sizeable enough to take care of the problem was $325,000 a year! There was no way he could afford that amount...but he didn't feel he could afford not to, either.

We took a little different approach with Bob. Since he had considerable wealth, and was in very good health, we pursued a premium financing option available to certain people. In order to make it work, we needed to find a product that could build cash value very quickly, so we chose a universal life contract that is indexed to several international markets.

We structured the policy to pay premiums for seven years at $750,000 a year. But since we are financing 90% of the premium, Bob only has to pay $75,000 a year.

Is it guaranteed? No, but it is very likely. And when you balance that against the fact that there is a 100% certainty that when he dies Uncle Sam will want eight million dollars of his money, and has the means to collect it, it isn't a bad gamble. In fact it was the only option he really had.

One very important thing you need to know about using life insurance for estate planning is you cannot do it with term insurance.

Term insurance is designed with one purpose only...to expire before you die. That is why it's so inexpensive. If you are using insurance for estate planning, you MUST use insurance that YOU KNOW will be there when you die. Otherwise you are taking a huge chance with your estate. And since your estate is everything you own, that means you are gambling 100% of everything you own AGAINST THE HOUSE, in this case, the insurance company.

You see, the insurance company does this for a living. Before they issue life insurance they look at everything they can find out about you. They look at your medical history, your family's background and history, your medical records. They talk to your doctors. They poke and prod you. They leave no stone uncovered.

Next they look at everything they can about the world you live in. They look at all the other people in your circumstances. People who have all the same stress factors, diseases, and similar family histories as you. They put it all together, crunch it in multi-million dollar computers. And then they make an offer.

And if it's term insurance you are buying, you can bet it was designed to expire. Probably the day before you die.

Ninety eight percent of term insurance policies never pay off. That means if you are purchasing a $100,000 policy that you have to pay $2,000 for, there is only a 2% chance it will pay off. In other words, you are paying $2,000 for a $2,000 payout.

You are better off to keep your money, and earn interest on it. Which is of course, just what the insurance company plans to do.

On the other hand, it if is costing you more than $2,000...say $4,000, you are being taken for a ride. The insurance company is making a killing. Do you really want to bet against these guys?

I wouldn't. And I wouldn't recommend you do, either. That's why it is so important to secure permanent insurance for your estate planning.

Does this mean that you should never use term insurance? Not at all. There are lots of cases where term is the appropriate choice. For example, you might have a mortgage that you want to pay off if you die. Term would be a great, and very inexpensive, answer.

Or, you might have been instructed by a divorce court to carry insurance on your life until your children reach the age of majority. Term once again, is an excellent choice for this. In other words, term insurance is great for events...or finite periods of time...or for a specific purpose.

Term is well defined, guaranteed for a specified term, and inexpensive. In these cases it's a perfect choice.

But if you want to guarantee you will be insured when you die, it is absolutely the wrong choice. And it's why we never provide term insurance for estate planning purpose unless we receive a letter from the client stating they know the chance they are taking, and are willing to hold us harmless in the event they die after the insurance has lapsed. And even with this provision, I can't think of a time when I have used it for this purpose.

Navigating Your Pension Choices

Here's another issue that is facing many Boomers. What should they do about their pensions?

Assume you are a healthy male, age 65, getting ready to retire. Your wife is 65, and also retired. Your HR manager informs you that you have several choices. The following are common choices provided by many pension plans:

- Take $60,000 a year for life (Life Only)

- Take $55,980 for life, with 10 years guaranteed (10-cc)

- Take $46,500 for your and your spouse's lifetimes (Joint and Survivor, or J&S).

Most retirees, of course choose the joint and survivor option. It's the easiest and apparently safest option, and HR administrators are often trained to suggest it. But this can be a costly mistake.

Let's look at various scenarios that can occur, and compare the J&S option with our Pension Max plan. Remember: the J&S decision is usually irrevocable; once made, it can't be changed.

Assume in all cases that the cost of taking the J&S option is: $60,000-$46,500=$13,500. Assume, too, that in the Pension Max a life policy of $589,000 is purchased on your life. This is enough to purchase an annuity that would provide $46,500 to your wife for the rest of her life if you were to die tomorrow, providing the same income as J&S. The following table shows several cases:

Scenario	Traditional Pension	Pension Max
You die at 76, spouse dies at 85 You both receive $46,500 income for the next 11 years. Then:	Your spouse continues to receive $46,5000 for another nine years. After spouse dies, all benefits expire. Heirs get nothing. Total Benefits: Retirement: 20 x 46.5k = $930k Benefit to heirs: 0 **Total Value : $930k**	When you die, your spouse uses the death benefit to purchase a life annuity that pays $1,000 per month more than she receives from the pension. She uses the difference to purchase a life insurance policy on her life with a death benefit of $385,000. Total Benefits: Retirement : 20 x 46.5k = 930k Benefit to heirs: $385k **Total Value: $1.35MM**
Spouse dies at 76, you die at 85 You both receive $46,500 income for the next 11 years. Then:	You continue to receive $46,500 for another nine years. After you die, all benefits expire. Heirs receive nothing. Total Benefits: Retirement: 20 x 46.5k = $930k Benefit to heirs: 0 **Total Value : $930k**	When your spouse dies, you can either take whatever cash value has built up in the life policy and have an income of $13,250 more per year, or keep the policy in force for your heirs. Either way worth more. Assume you keep the policy: Total Benefits: Retirement: 20 x 46.5k=$930k Benefit to heirs: $589k **Total Value: $1.52MM**
You both die at same time, assume 20 years out.	You both receive $46,500 for the next 20 years, and then income stops when you both die. Total Benefits: Retirement: 20 x 46.5k = $930k Benefit to heirs: 0 **Total Value : $930k**	You both receive $46,500 for the next 20 years. Then death benefit pays out to your heirs. Total Benefits: Retirement: 20 x 46.5k=$930k Benefit to heirs: $589k **Total Value: $1.52MM**
Now assume 10 years out.	You both receive $46,500 for the next 10 years, and then income stops when you both die. Retirement: 10 x 46.5k = $465k Benefit to heirs: 0 **Total Value : $465k**	You both receive $46,500 for the next 20 years. Then death benefit pays out to your heirs. Retirement: 10 x 46.5k=$465k Benefit to heirs: $589k **Total Value : $1.054MM**

Note that in all cases, the Pension Max plan is worth more. Why? First look at the original plan proposed by your HR manager. Remember the cost of the Joint and Survivor plan:

$60,000 (the amount you get for your life only)
- $46,500 (the amount you get for you and spouse)
$13,500 (the amount you pay for the J&S option)

So you are paying $13,500 a year to protect your spouse in case you die before she does. What's another name for buying financial protection for your loved ones in case you die?

Life Insurance! That's right. That $13,500 is a PREMIUM exacted by the pension plan to extend payments to your spouse after you die. Otherwise, if you just took the $60,000 per year, it would end on your death, leaving nothing for your spouse.

Okay, so now that you know that you are actually purchasing life insurance with your $13,500 premium, why don't we compare it with other products on the market? After all, if you were purchasing life insurance from an agent, wouldn't you compare products?

At age 65, if you were a non-smoking male in good health, what could $13,500 per year buy?

A Preferred Non-Tobacco rating with one of the premier life companies in the world would provide a policy with a death benefit of $642,761. If you got a Standard rating with the same company, you would be able to purchase a policy with a death benefit of $506,249.

Okay, now assume you live to life expectancy, which is age 82. Upon your death, your wife who is also 82 receives $506,249, INCOME TAX FREE. Under the standard J&S pension plan, she would continue to receive the $46,500 (fully taxed) annually until she dies. However, under the pension max plan, she could use the $506,249 to purchase a life annuity that would provide income of $69,670 every year for the rest of her life. And since the income is derived from a Single Premium Immediate Annuity (SPIA), it is 92% tax free! So the difference in net income for your spouse, assuming she is in the 15% tax bracket, is $29,309 per year:

$$(69,671 \times (1-(0.08*0.15))) - (46,500 \times .85) = \$29,309$$

That's nearly $30,000 more per year in net income! Just for shopping the life insurance, instead of purchasing it from the pension company. And with NO RISK whatsoever.

However, instead of keeping the extra $29,309 your spouse could elect to purchase a SPIA that pays out the $46,500 she would have gotten under the traditional pension plan. That would only cost $337,918. And she gets to keep the balance of $168,000! That's money you have created by choosing Pension Max rather than the traditional Joint and Survivor option. By buying smart.

What happens if she dies before you? In the traditional plan, you would be stuck with the lower payout of $46,500 for the rest of your life. But with the Pension Max plan, you would have the option of cashing in the life policy, collecting the cash value, and enjoying the higher income for the rest of your life.

Or you could keep the policy and pass it along to your kids. Either way, it's up to you...because YOU control the life policy, not the pension company!

Does this always work? No. You may not be insurable when you retire, or you may be insurable, but have a health impairment that reduces your death benefit to a point where it wouldn't work. Or the cost of the joint and survivor option might be substantially less than the cost of life insurance (it happens).

But if you are healthy, and you are expecting a pension, you owe it to yourself, as well as your loved ones, to explore different options. That's where a good wealth preservation planner comes in.

So why isn't this done more often? First, HR professionals are not trained to do this, and that's who people often turn to for help with these pension decisions.

Also, people generally think life insurance is only for young families to provide for spouses and children if the breadwinner dies. That isn't their fault; it's the fault of the industry which has done a poor job of getting the word out.

Also, people don't like to think about it, and life insurance agents are often times setting people up with the wrong product or the wrong policy for their situation, just to get them covered. For example, many agents sell term insurance because it's an easy sell and seems less expensive to their clients.

However, if you look at the long term, a permanent policy that is guaranteed to pay benefits is generally much less expensive than a term life policy, which only pays benefits 2% of the time.

If it's structured correctly in the right situation, life insurance can be very powerful. It can cut out the lawyers and the IRS. It can be a legacy builder. And when it's done right... **it can be free!**

Insurance is one of the most potent tools we have in income and estate planning, and everyone needs it at some time or another.

In a nutshell, insurance let's you spread your risk of just about anything among the general population, and that can be a huge advantage.

Home Equity:
Safe Harbor or Leaky Boat?

Many people have worked hard all their lives to pay off the mortgages in their homes. They believe by doing so they have made their retirements much more secure. People tell me this all the time.

However, for many people this simply is not true. And it's one of the most difficult things to explain to people. So let's take a moment to understand why equity in your home is not necessarily a Safe Harbor.

First, does the equity in your home earn interest for you? No. Not a dime. Not one red cent. "Wait a minute," you say. "Ten years ago my home was only worth $250,000, but today it's worth almost $400,000. Isn't that growth?"

Yes. It is. But it has nothing to do with whether or not you paid off your mortgage...it has to do with the growth in value of your home. Your home value would be worth $400,000 today whether you paid off your mortgage or not.

Now what happened to the money that you put into the house? Nothing. It's still sitting there earning no interest and exposed to all kinds of storms. "What storms?" you ask.

How about taxes? Is the money you paid into your home doing anything for you on the taxation front? Once again, the answer is no. The money in your home is sitting idle, not helping you at all. In fact, by not paying a mortgage, you may be losing out on one of the most powerful tax benefits there is…the interest deduction on a mortgage payment. Further, if you sell your home, you may be subject to capital gains taxes…once again whether you owe money on it or not.

What about creditors? Is the money you have tied up in your home safe from creditors, lawsuits, nursing homes, etc.? Of course not. In fact it's one of the primary targets for these individuals if you run afoul of them. Your home is the first thing they go after. It's the most visible and obvious asset you have. And the worst part of that is, if they are successful and manage to assume ownership of it, you and your loved ones are without a place to live!

Is the money that's tied up in your home safe from inflation? Well the value of the home tends to rise to keep pace with inflation, but once again, that happens whether you owe money on it or not. So you don't really add to the value of that holding by having your money tied up in your home.

How about the probate storm? Is your home safe from probate? Unless you have put your home in trust, it will go through probate. And worse yet, if you own real estate in more than one state, your estate will have to go through multiple probates.

How about risk? Surely your home value is secure, correct? It's one of the safest places to put your money? At the time of this writing we are going through the biggest mortgage crisis since the Great Depression and one of the most serious real estate corrections we have ever experienced.

In my own middle class residential neighborhood in my beautiful New England town (named the Best Place to Live in America twice in recent years) we have two bank foreclosures sitting right on my street. One is right next door. The lawn doesn't get mowed, the paper doesn't get picked up, and we don't know what is happening on the inside. But what I do know is it isn't helping the value of my home at all. In fact, all of the gains we have experienced over the past five years have nearly disappeared. So no, the market value of your home is not secure either. In fact, it can be very vulnerable to the risk storm.

So we now see that the home is not a Safe Harbor from our main storms. But what about other things we haven't even considered. For example, what about liquidity? Is the money you have tied up in your home liquid?

Not at all. In order to access the money you have in your home you will have to borrow against it, if you can qualify! When you do this, you give away your rights to do other things with the home, such as sell it or give it away or borrow more money… unless you first clear up the note on the house or receive permission from the lender.

And all of that, of course, is assuming the lender is willing to lend you the money in the first place! Some banker (who is probably spooked by all the bad loans his bank made over the last several years) has to say you are worthy of using your own money! And he's going to charge you for the privilege.

Further, many home equity lines of credit already approved and in place have been frozen during the recent home mortgage crisis. Some have even been called (what would happen to you if a bank called a loan you were depending on to live?).

Many people who were depending on the equity in their homes to live have found that to be unavailable to them at a time when they need it the most.

So what am I saying? That you shouldn't own a home? Of course not. Home ownership in the United States is one of the key reasons – perhaps the *key* reason – the American middle class has become the most vital economic power the world has ever seen. It is crucial to our way of life.

All I am saying is just because you own your home – and perhaps have it paid off – it doesn't mean your money is in the most efficient or safest harbor available. In fact, a more accurate description might be a leaky barrel that is bobbing along in the ocean... just out of reach and subject to all the storms the sea can throw at it. In other words, it's completely exposed to nearly everything... except perhaps your ability to use it!

And worse yet, for many people the wealth stored in their homes is the most significant asset they have. Many, in fact, viewed their homes as their retirement plans. Far too many of those people are now paying the price for very poor planning.

Life Boats In the Storm

So what can you do that might be a more valuable use of your money? Well, there are a couple of things. First, if you are 62 or older, you may want to consider a reverse mortgage. A reverse mortgage allows people who are 62 or older to convert part of the equity in their home to tax free income without having to give up title or take on a monthly payment.

In order to qualify, you must be at least 62 years of age, own and have 40% or more equity in your home, and it must be your primary residence. Health, net worth, income, and credit scores are not a factor. The only thing that is looked at is the equity in your home and the age of the youngest owner.

No income restrictions are imposed. Whether you are near destitute or a multi-millionaire, you are entitled to tap the unused equity in your home for whatever purpose you choose. Ability to pay is not a factor; you do not have to qualify either financially or health wise. You must only be at least 62 years old and owner of the home as your principal residence.

An appraisal is required as the value of your home will be a factor in the amount of money available to you. An attorney, on the other hand, is not required but we strongly encourage you to seek advice from a legal, tax or financial advisor before committing to a reverse mortgage. Note: Uncle Charlie is NOT a good advisor.

Other costs are very similar to those associated with standard mortgages. The charges will include an appraisal fee, termite inspection, origination fee, mortgage insurance fee (for FHA/HUD mortgages, other standard recording or closing costs, etc. In most instances these fees are capped, financed as part of the reverse mortgage and taken out of the loan proceeds at the closing, so there is no out of pocket cost to you.

The amount of money you can borrow depends upon your age, market value and equity in the home and the interest rate at the time of origination, as well as the type of loan. Typically, the older you are, the more you can borrow. Government (HUD) loans are capped at a lower rate than so called jumbo loans available through private lenders. For homes with equity up to $500,000 this is usually not an issue. But if you have a home worth more than that, you may want to visit with a private lender about a jumbo loan.

If you already have a mortgage on your home, it will be paid off from the proceeds of the reverse mortgage loan. Your reverse mortgage will then be based upon the remaining equity.

Proceeds from a reverse mortgage are not taxable; it's your money (equity), not taxable income. Nor will your regular Social Security or Medicare be affected. The impact, if any, on other federal, state or local assistance programs should be discussed with your financial advisor or the program sponsor.

Reverse mortgages are very flexible. You can choose to receive fixed monthly payments for as long as the home is your primary residence, a lump sum payment, a line of credit, or any combination of the above. Since the program is backed by the US government, you will never owe more than the value of your home – even if you receive monthly payments for the next 20 or 30 years! Finally, you keep title to your property – it stays part of your estate.

You can never outlive the loan. If you end up borrowing more than the value of the house because you lived a long life, or because the home lost value in a down market, the worse that can happen is the bank sells your home and the difference is made up from insurance. Your estate will never be required to make up any balance. However, if when you leave the home or die there is equity left after the loan is repaid, that does go back to you or your estate. Simply put, there is no risk involved with using a reverse mortgage to tap the value of your equity.

Further, there are no restrictions on what you can use the money for. You can pay off medical bills, purchase or pay for health insurance or health care, life insurance, repair your home, purchase a second home, pay for college tuition for your grandchildren, travel, put it in the bank or use it any way you choose.

One of the primary concerns of seniors is who owns the home after a reverse mortgage is taken out. Nothing changes. Just like in the case of a regular mortgage, you will continue to own and have title to your home.

Unlike in a conventional mortgage, payments are not made to the lender; the lending institution pays you. As long as at least one of

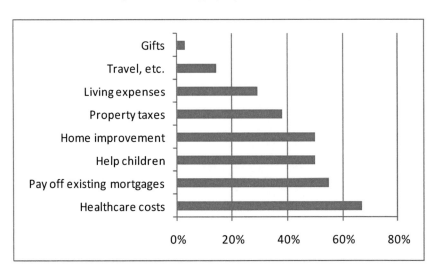

Figure 7: Most common uses for reverse mortgages

the primary residents continues to occupy the home as their primary residence, you are only responsible for maintaining your home and paying for insurance and property taxes.

What Happens When You Leave?

You may leave your home for periods of under one year. Non-occupancy of your principal residence for more than one year will cause the reverse mortgage to become due. So if you have a winter home in Florida or a summer home in the Maine, you will still be able to enjoy it, as long as you live in your home for part of each year.

If you are married and one of you passes away, the other may continue to stay in the home and receive the income derived from the reverse mortgage. Once the last primary resident vacates the home, the loan must be repaid. The loan must be repaid when the home is no longer the primary residence of the owner, the home is sold, or the last owner dies.

If all owners do pass away, the loan becomes due. If there is little or no value left in the home, it can go back to the bank. The bank will sell the home and refund any balances due to the estate. However, if less than the loan is recouped, your estate is not responsible for this mortgage.

If there is excess value in the home the trustees or executor may prefer to manage the sale themselves, as sometimes banks will simply move a property for the amount owed, or close to it, since they have to return the excess to the estate. The estate has 12 months to repay the loan, so there is time to determine the best way to do it. Again, they keep the excess proceeds of the sale after satisfying the mortgage.

The estate or heirs may also choose to repay the balance due on the reverse mortgage and keep the home. The only requirement is that the loan be satisfied in as much as there is value left in the property.

Let's look at a few examples, assuming home equity of $250,000. The following table shows what you would receive at various ages if you were to take a lump sum or lifetime income. FYI, you can also mix and match, taking partial lump sums with the rest in income, etc. Also, lump sums will grow by 4.4% per year if not accessed immediately.

Age	Home Equity	Lump Sum	Lifetime Income
62	250000	$140,725	$786/mo
65	250000	$146,854	$840/mo
70	250000	$157,379	$951/mo
75	250000	$168,500	$1,100/mo

Reverse mortgages are not necessarily for everyone. For example if you have little equity (less than 40%), or were planning to be in the home for less than two or three years, you may not wish to do one. You should always consult with a qualified professional before making any decisions.

But you should NOT BE AFRAID. Reverse mortgages can be wonderful answers to the problem of how to access your most valuable source of wealth. And for many, they can mean the difference between struggling and a comfortable retirement.

Equity Harvesting

Another way of tapping into the value of your home is known as "Equity Harvesting." Books have been written on this, including a major national best seller. The purpose of *this* book is not to give you an in-depth look at this technique (or any other). But we will scratch the surface and give an overview of the process.

Most equity harvesting strategies employ a conventional home equity loan (though a reverse mortgage can also be used) along with another, no-risk, tax-free investment.

Some programs and books make references to special acronyms or terms to describe these financial instruments. But no matter what they call them, they are always talking about cash value life insurance. The reason? Cash value life insurance is the only way to grow your money tax deferred and take it out tax free…unless you utilize a Roth IRA. The problem with a Roth is that it cannot be funded all at once unless you are converting a conventional IRA, so it is not a good way to go for equity harvesting, or anything else that needs to be rapidly funded.

So how does it work? A homeowner will take out a line of credit on their home and then use it to *overfund* a permanent cash-value life policy. These are usually fixed index Universal Life insurance policies. A fixed indexed universal life policy is similar to the Fixed Indexed Annuities described later in this book. The main difference is that they carry a death benefit greater than the amount of cash buildup (whereas a Fixed Annuity will pay the full value of the annuity on death). That's important, because when you take money out of a cash value life policy, it comes out income tax free as long as it is "borrowed" and there is a death benefit large enough to pay back the "loan." Again, this is the ONLY way to do this.

So let's look at a hypothetical case. Assume you are a 50 year old male non-smoker in good health and have a $600,000 home with $300,000 in equity that you want to "harvest." You would take out a home owner's equity line of credit for $180,000 (keep it under 80% to keep interest costs low), at 6% interest. Each year for 15 years you extract 1/15th, or $12,000 and use it to fund a fixed indexed universal life policy for $100,000. We keep it low so cash will build fast.

Here is an illustration for that life insurance policy, funded with $12,000 per year:

End of Year	Age	Annual Premium	Cash from Policy	Taxes Due	Cash from Policy Less Tax	Surr. Cash Value Increase	Non-Guaranteed Assumed Surr. Cash Value	Death Benefit
1	51	12,000	0	0	0	7,740	7,740	100,000
2	52	12,000	0	0	0	12,721	20,461	100,000
3	53	12,000	0	0	0	13,729	34,190	100,000
4	54	12,000	0	0	0	14,767	48,957	120,296
5	55	12,000	0	0	0	15,851	64,808	151,735
6	56	12,000	0	0	0	17,017	81,825	183,821
7	57	12,000	0	0	0	18,263	100,088	216,635
8	58	12,000	0	0	0	19,614	119,701	250,276
9	59	12,000	0	0	0	21,057	140,758	284,824
10	60	12,000	0	0	0	23,729	164,487	322,553
		120,000	0	0	0	164,487		
11	61	12,000	0	0	0	25,904	190,391	362,273
12	62	12,000	0	0	0	28,013	218,404	403,663
13	63	12,000	0	0	0	30,300	248,703	446,915
14	64	12,000	0	0	0	32,781	281,484	492,244
15	65	12,000	0	0	0	35,472	316,956	539,891
16	66	0	25,000	6,684	18,316	-651	316,305	542,885
17	67	0	25,000	7,149	17,851	-674	315,631	546,001
18	68	0	25,000	7,646	17,354	-384	315,247	549,328
19	69	0	25,000	8,178	16,822	-71	315,176	552,772
20	70	0	25,000	8,746	16,254	241	315,417	556,265
		180,000	125,000	38,404	86,596	315,417		
21	71	0	25,000	9,354	15,646	546	315,963	559,828
22	72	0	25,000	10,005	14,995	864	316,827	563,755
23	73	0	25,000	10,700	14,300	1,214	318,041	567,583
24	74	0	25,000	11,444	13,556	1,617	319,658	571,664
25	75	0	25,000	12,240	12,760	2,109	321,766	576,299

Notice that by year 15 you've accumulated $316,956 in cash value, with a death benefit of $549,891. If anything happens to you, your family is very well protected. Note, too, how you can begin to take $25,000 a year, tax free, at age 65, and you will be able to continue to take that for the rest of your life, without reducing the death benefit.

You may be wondering about the "Taxes Due" column. This only comes into play if the policy should lapse before you die. If you hold this policy for life, you receive the entire death benefit without having to pay any taxes. So we design the policy so it cannot collapse; should you ever take so much it is about to, it will automatically convert to a guaranteed life death benefit with no cash value. This protects you from ever having to pay income taxes!

Following is the second half of this report, depicting ages 76-100:

End of Year	Age	Annual Premium	Cash from Policy	Taxes Due	Cash from Policy Less Tax	Surr. Cash Value Increase	Non-Guaranteed Assumed Surr. Cash Value	Death Benefit
26	76	0	25,000	13,090	11,910	2,602	324,368	581,353
27	77	0	25,000	14,000	11,000	3,207	327,575	586,953
28	78	0	25,000	14,974	10,026	3,842	331,417	593,110
29	79	0	25,000	16,015	8,985	4,496	335,913	599,626
30	80	0	25,000	17,128	7,872	5,173	341,086	606,443
		180,000	375,000	167,353	207,647	341,086		
31	81	0	25,000	18,319	6,681	5,915	347,001	613,539
32	82	0	25,000	19,592	5,408	6,693	353,694	621,185
33	83	0	25,000	20,954	4,046	7,588	361,282	629,454
34	84	0	25,000	22,411	2,589	8,581	369,864	638,647
35	85	0	25,000	23,969	1,031	9,644	379,508	649,087
36	86	0	25,000	25,635	-635	10,751	390,258	660,826
37	87	0	25,000	27,417	-2,417	11,905	402,164	673,562
38	88	0	25,000	29,323	-4,323	13,146	415,309	687,654
39	89	0	25,000	31,362	-6,362	14,493	429,802	702,569
40	90	0	25,000	33,542	-8,542	16,031	445,833	718,090
		180,000	625,000	419,878	205,122	445,833		
41	91	0	0	29,189	-29,189	44,588	490,421	760,937
42	92	0	0	31,219	-31,219	48,825	539,246	805,706
43	93	0	0	33,389	-33,389	53,749	592,995	852,469
44	94	0	0	35,710	-35,710	59,525	652,521	899,906
45	95	0	0	38,193	-38,193	66,551	719,072	948,355
46	96	0	0	40,848	-40,848	74,419	793,491	997,214
47	97	0	0	43,687	-43,687	83,980	877,470	1,047,208
48	98	0	0	46,724	-46,724	96,436	973,906	1,102,086
49	99	0	0	49,973	-49,973	112,457	1,086,364	1,168,347
50	100	0	0	53,447	-53,447	132,403	1,218,767	1,307,570
		180,000	625,000	822,256	-197,256	1,218,767		

Here, you see that in spite of continuing to take the $25,000 per year until age 90, your cash value continues to grow as does your death benefit.

In fact you could take more than the $25,000 per year as time goes on...consider it an inflation hedge. Further, if you ever need a large pool of cash, you could take it from the cash value, as long as the policy does not lapse and you die with it in force.

That's the key. By paying off the loan with the death benefit, you avoid paying any income taxes for the money you took from the policy. Finally, whenever you do die, your heirs will receive the full death benefit. Assuming life expectancy (age 82), they would receive $621,000.

So, the total amount harvested from your equity was:

$441,000	(Death benefit less $180,000 loan)
425,000	($25,000 income for 17 years)
$866,000	(Total Received)

Total amount paid over 32 years:

$280,800   (Interest – tax deductible)

The net return on your investment in zero-risk tax free income:

7.21%.

However if you figure in the amount you saved on income taxes from deducting your interest payments, you made a return of 9.08%. In tax free income.

To put that in perspective, to make an equivalent tax free return of 9.08% in the market, you would have to have a taxable return of 12.6%.

NOT including fees! Or risk! Or any of those other things we dislike so much.

So simply by putting your equity to work for you, you are able to realize a net, after tax return equivalent to more than 12.6%! Without any risk or fees. Let me say that again. With NO MARKET RISK and NO FEES.

And as an added benefit, you were able to cover your loved ones with a rock-solid life insurance policy that would have paid off handsomely if you had died early. Now that's a double-win, and a true Safe Harbor! And it's only possible with life insurance!

Do you still have questions about why we like it so much?

The Truth About Annuities and How They Keep You Safe

What if there were a place where you could put your money that

- Is 100% FREE OF MARKET RISK,

- Provides a REASONABLE RATE OF RETURN,

- Incurs NO FEES,

- Grows TAX-DEFERRED and may pay TAX FREE income,

- Provides MINIMUM GUARANTEED RETURNS,

- PROVIDES even GREATER RETURNS when the stock market goes up,

- PRESERVES ALL PRINCIPAL AND INTEREST when the market goes down,

- Can provide GUARANTEED LIFETIME income,

- Is backed and managed by the SAFEST FINANCIAL INDUSTRY in history, with over $2,797,582,000,000 *(2.8 trillion dollars)* in assets backing it up?

Well they exist, and many planners won't even consider them because they are different types of life insurance and annuity contracts. That's right; life insurance and annuities.

And they are way too often dismissed as unimportant, trivial, or even bad by investors, the news media, and financial planners.

Why is that? I don't really know, because they are remarkable instruments that offer features nothing else does (more about that in a minute).

But I have my suspicions, and it goes back to those fees.

I have an acquaintance who is a financial planner and money manager. We were talking about each other's business one day over lunch. I was lauding the advantages of insurance and annuities to my clients, and he said something very revealing to me.

He said that he uses insurance sometimes, but really doesn't like it that much. When I asked him why he said, "because it doesn't fit my business model."

When I asked him to elaborate he said, "My management fees are ongoing. It's my retirement strategy. When I get up in the morning, I have a steady income. When you get up every morning, you have to start over...every day. That's too much work for me. And face it...insurance just isn't that sexy" (actual quote!).

Accumulation vs. Speculation

Perhaps the main reason fixed insurance products work so well is that principal is never put at risk. As long as you fulfill the terms of the contract, your principal is protected. Your money is in very safe accounts, such as U.S. government and investment grade bonds.

In fact, they may be the safest accounts in history. It's the truth: during the Great Depression when banks were failing and people could not get their money from their stock brokers, banks or S&Ls, where did they turn? You guessed it...fixed annuities and life insurance!

Another reason is because insurance is unique in all the world. It's the only way you can guarantee you will have a tax-free pool of liquid cash available, exactly when and where you need it at the most important of times, that can't be tied up by creditors, probate, the legal system, nursing homes, etc.

Everyone's financial plan should include life insurance. Insurance and annuities provide wonderful benefits that many retirees are unaware of.

Malcolm Forbes, who had $40 million in life insurance when he died, was reported to have said that if he'd known what a great bargain it was, he would have had twice that amount!

And Ben Bernanke, Chairman of the Federal Reserve, is said to hold 100% of his retirement in annuities.

Financial Magic?

No risk. No fees. Tax deferral or tax elimination. Guaranteed lifetime income. How can this be?

Is it alchemy? Is it magic? Is it legal? Is it sexy? Nope...nope... absolutely, and, well, WE think so! And it's completely legal and above board for one reason only: Surrender Charges.

When a contract is sold by a life insurance company and has a fixed duration and a surrender charge for early withdrawals, it comes under the special tax laws reserved for insurance products, which allows for these special benefits.

Now I know what you're thinking. You're thinking you don't want to have anything to do with anything that has surrender charges. They are bad. They are evil. You know this because your Uncle Charlie told you so. But are they really?

Surrender charges are really no more than part of an agreement between you and the insurance company. If you agree to allow it to use your money for a predetermined period of time, the insurance company gives you guarantees you can bank on and accepts all the costs and risk and charges no fees. If you withdraw your money early they simply ask you to cover the costs they incurred on the portion you withdrew. Further, these charges are graduated...the longer you leave the money in, the lower they will be.

And since the charge is completely spelled out, it's easy to plan for. It would never be wise for you to put all your money in one of these plans...just what you want to defer for a later time, and grow tax deferred without fees. The rest should probably be put in more liquid accounts, such as money market accounts, CDs, bonds, funds, etc. Then you never ever have to worry about surrender charges!

But if an emergency does arise, you have the option of withdrawing up to 10% a year without penalties. And if you should die, become terminally ill, or require nursing care...the full value of your principal plus interest is paid to you or your heirs without charges.

So, are surrender charges bad? You tell me. Take a look at the facing page. It outlines what the insurance company is really saying when they impose surrender charges...and what the mutual fund company is saying when they don't. Then you decide how bad they really are.

Insurance Company	Mutual Fund Company
Lend us your money for a certain period of time (1...2...5...7...10 years). We promise to pay it back, plus interest, at the end of the term.	We take your money and gamble it on securities. We promise to do our best, but if we lose it, it's gone. Less the fees, of course.
We take all the risk. Your principal, guaranteed rate of return, and earned interest is never in doubt.	You take all the risk. No guarantees on principal. No guarantees on return. 100% guarantee on fees.
If market conditions allow, your return could be much better, but never worse than the guaranteed rate. You are never locked into a fixed rate of return.	If the market goes up, we will pass along your earnings, less fees and taxes. But if the market goes down, you lose (but we don't take risks...our fees come off the top!).
Once interest is earned, it accrues to your account and is guaranteed regardless of market conditions.	Only fees are guaranteed, never earnings and growth. Could be here today and gone tomorrow.
No fees. 100% of your money compounds annually for your benefit.	Fees guaranteed...right off the top! Can take as much as 80% of your profits (see page 30).
Taxes deferred. Again 100% of your money compounds for your benefit.	Taxes whether you make money or not. In fact, if we have a losing year, you are probably going to pay more taxes. Average tax costs on mutual funds: 44% of earnings (page 15).
If you do need to take money out early we will need to ask you to cover our expenses on the portion you withdraw. This will be laid out in advance, with no surprises, so you will be able to plan.	You may withdraw your current balance at any time. This is subject to market gains and losses, fees and taxes. There are no surrender charges...but we have been extracting fees the entire time we had your money, so please don't worry about us.
We understand that unexpected things come up, so we will allow you to withdraw up to 10% a year penalty free. And if you die, become terminally ill, or go into a nursing home, we pay you or your heirs the full accumulated value, including interest, no questions asked.	Good luck with that. If the market is up, you win. If not...well so sorry. Oh, and don't forget our fees. We love those fees!

Who Buys Life Insurance and Annuities?

Don't take my word for it. Take a look at what the professionals say and do:

- Any time there is a structured settlement or payout, such as in all state lotteries, court awarded settlements, school teacher and state pension plans, non-profit entities, churches, and many others, <u>professional money managers employ annuities</u>.

- According to a recent article in the Wall Street Journal Online:

  "(A) study, soon to be released by the University of Pennsylvania's Wharton Financial Institutions Center, finds that so-called income annuities can assure retirees of an income stream for life at a cost as much as 40% less than a traditional stock, bond and cash mix.

  "...What it means is that retirees who need a nest egg of, say, $1 million, <u>can live the same lifestyle with as little as $600,000 in an income annuity</u>.

  "...That news could offer hope for the millions of workers about to retire with inadequate retirement savings...." *

- Ben Bernanke, Chairman of the Federal Reserve, is reported to hold 100% of his retirement holdings in annuities!

Historical Performance, Worst, Middle and Best

On the facing page is an independent analysis of fixed indexed annuity returns derived by using an independent computer modeling program. The model looked at a sample of 200 historical 15-year time periods from 1975 to the present.

Opdyke, Jeff D., "The Case for 'Income Annuities'," *The Wall Street Journal Online,* August 13, 2007

Duration	Worst 1/25/1976 Account Value	Worst 1/25/1976 Annualized Return	Middle 11/20/1990 Account Value	Middle 11/20/1990 Annualized Return	Best 8/19/1982 Account Value	Best 8/19/1982 Annualized Return
0	$100,000	N/A	$100,000	N/A	$100,000	N/A
1	$100,963	0.96%	$113,038	13.04%	$135,665	35.66%
2	$100,963	0.00%	$121,554	7.53%	$135,665	0.00%
3	$108,940	7.90%	$126,805	4.32%	$146,738	8.16%
4	$116,790	7.21%	$126,805	0.00%	$179,309	22.20%
5	$127,268	8.97%	$152,169	20.00%	$221,177	23.35%
6	$127,268	0.00%	$177,253	16.48%	$221,177	0.00%
7	$146,507	15.12%	$212,133	19.68%	$271,438	22.72%
8	$161,476	10.22%	$241,829	14.00%	$271,438	0.00%
9	$167,437	3.69%	$277,280	14.66%	$296,214	9.13%
10	$184,679	10.30%	$277,280	0.00%	$314,909	6.31%
11	$223,707	21.13%	$277,280	0.00%	$330,208	4.86%
12	$223,707	0.00%	$277,280	0.00%	$330,208	0.00%
13	$243,830	9.00%	$298,919	7.80%	$374,627	13.45%
14	$262,317	7.58%	$322,587	7.92%	$421,082	12.40%
15	$263,098	0.30%	$332,246	2.99%	$535,573	27.19%

Annualized Rate of Return over term (15 years)	6.66%	8.33%	11.84%

Figure 8: Best, worst and middle 15 year Safe Harbor periods 1975-2007

In other words, the worst performance was 6.66%, the average was 8.33%, and the best was 11.84% over 15 years...*with no market risk, fees or taxes.*

Below is a comparison of fixed indexed annuities, the S&P 500 and historical CD rates for 1973 through 2006.

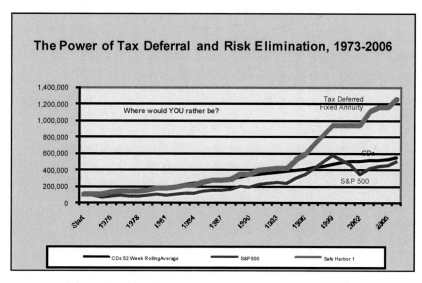

Figure 9: Sexy indeed! Shows how tax-deferred growth accounts with no risk or fees can outpace the market.

Peeking Under the Hood

So how, exactly, do Fixed Indexed Annuities work? How can they "magically" provide upside in the market with no downside? Isn't this too good to be true?

One might certainly think so. Let's take a look "under the hood" and see if we can clear it up a bit.

First, money that is used to purchase indexed annuities is never invested in the stock market. This is a key difference between an indexed annuity and a variable annuity. When you put money into a variable annuity, it is allocated to individual "sub-accounts" that are used to purchase securities in the market. When those securities go up in value, you make money; when they go down, you lose. In order to mitigate those losses and make them more palatable to conservative investors, insurance companies often load them up with riders like guaranteed death benefits (basically life insurance that you pay for), guaranteed income riders, etc.

But all of these riders cost money in the form of fees. In fact it's not uncommon to see variable annuities with fees of 3% or more. To put that in perspective, if you put $250,000 into a variable annuity for 10 years, you would be charged fees of about $75,000! Wouldn't you really rather keep that money for yourself?

An indexed annuity is a completely different animal. The money you put into that annuity is never invested in the stock market. Rather, it goes into the general fund of the insurance company, and is invested in fixed money instruments, just the same as all of the life and fixed annuity premium is. In other words, it is only in the very safest low risk investments available. And it's backed up by the same State Guaranty Fund that backs up all insurance dollars.

Historically these funds average about 4% return annually. The insurance company takes its profits operating margins right off the top; and that consumes about 2% annually.

A lot of people wonder how this can be enough for these big insurance companies. Surely, there must be a catch. But remember, the insurance company is making this off YOUR money...not its own. So it collects millions and millions of dollars, puts it in a safe money investment, and makes 2%. You and I would be happy to do that all day long.

But that brings us to the surrender charges. See, to set up an annuity and pay marketing and overhead costs generally costs the insurance company about 10% for the average 10 year annuity. That's why there is a surrender fee. As long as you keep it until the end of the term, there are no charges. All of your money goes to earning tax-deferred interest with no fees. But if you pull out early, the insurance company has to recapture its outlay.

Okay; you've given the insurance company your money, it puts it into an account that earns on average around 4% annually, the insurance company takes 2% off the top. What's that leave for you? Right, around 2%. But no one would tie up their money for 10 years for a paltry 2% return, right?

So the insurance company takes that 2% and buys options in the market. Options are a contract that gives the purchaser of the option the right (but NOT the obligation) to purchase a security sometime in the future at a given price. So assume a security is selling today for $10 and the insurance company buys an option to purchase that security 12 months from now at today's price. If 12 months from now it was selling on the market for $11, then that $10 option is a great buy. The annuity company can purchase as much stock as it purchased options for at $10 and immediately turn around and sell it for $11. That's an immediate return of $1 per option share. That money is then passed along to you in the form of interest earned on your annuity.

If the market goes up even more, then the value of the option is even higher. Say the index hit $12. Now that's a profit of $2 per share. So now the insurance company can afford to pay you more in interest! The higher the market goes, the more you earn.

But what happens if the market goes down? How much do you lose? Well, how much of your money is actually in the market? None...right? Your money is in the general fund of the life insurance company that is invested in very conservative and safe money investments and backed up by the State Guaranty Fund. It's 100% safe. You haven't lost a dime.

Remember, the insurance company purchased the OPTION to purchase a security at a given price...not the OBLIGATION to. So, if the market goes down, the purchaser of the options simply lets them expire. They aren't worth anything. But there's no damage done, either, because the money used to purchase the options was budgeted out of the difference between what your money is earning in the insurance company's general fund, and what the insurance company took to cover its costs and profits. So if the options aren't worth anything, you simply don't receive any interest...but you didn't LOSE anything either!

Okay, so now you should understand where the money comes from to pay you the interest if the market goes up, and why your money is protected if the market goes down. But it doesn't tell you the full story.

See, options cost more when markets are volatile than they do when markets are steady. Also, the bonds and other fixed investments the insurance company invests your money in might earn more or less than four percent. If the options cost a lot, or interest rates are down, the insurance company must buy fewer options (remember there is a fixed amount available to purchase them). If options are selling at a bargain, the insurance company can buy more.

The quantity of options the insurance company can purchase determines the amount of interest it can pay you if the market goes up. So, there are limits on the amount of interest you can be paid.

These limits take the form of "moving parts" in the annuity's "crediting strategy." These moving parts can take the form of "caps," "spreads," "participation rates," etc. All of them limit the amount of interest that's paid if the market goes up.

So, looking at the previous example. Assume the market is very volatile and options are expensive, so caps are relative low...say 6.5%. That means that no matter how high the market goes, you can only earn 6.5%. So if it goes up 2%, you earn 2%. If it goes up 4%, you earn 4%. But if it goes up 10%, you earn 6.5%.

If, however, the market were steady, the price of options should go down. So now the insurance company can purchase more. Now the cap might be 9%, or 12%, or even higher. So, if the market goes up 10%, you could earn the entire 10...or even more. We've seen people earn as much as 18 or even 20% a year...but we've also seen them earn zero.

The important thing to understand is that it's ALL MARKET DRIVEN. Some people believe that if the market went up 10 and the cap was set at six, the insurance company is pocketing the other four. That is NOT how it works. The insurance company got its two off the top, and that's all it will get, regardless of what happens. If the cost of options goes down and the insurance company can afford to buy more, the caps will be higher and the potential for you to earn more goes up. But you are NEVER at risk of losing your principal.

Okay, so the market went up 10 and you got 6.5...now what? Now your annuity is worth 6.5% more than it was before. It can never go down from that unless you take money out. Next year the company purchases more options, resets caps and spreads, and the market does what it will do. If it goes up you earn. If it goes down, your principal *and* the 6.5% interest are safe.

One more thing. Since you didn't lose anything when the market went down, you have nothing to make up once the market starts up again. So you are always either going up or staying steady. To see what this can mean to you, take another look at Figure 10 on page 79.

Market-Like Returns Without The Risk

By now you should understand *how* FIAs (fixed indexed annuities) do what they do, but you still may be fuzzy on why all of this is so important to you. This section is going to cover what all of this means to you and your bottom line, and how powerful they can be for you. Some of this is repetition from prior sections, but a little repetition can be helpful...especially when put another way.

Consider this quote by Donald Trump from "The Art of the Deal": "As long as the basic concept remained intact—no downside for me and a 50% share in the upside—it was an extraordinary deal." This is the basis of what fixed indexed annuities do for you...they eliminate the downside and give you a portion (often around 50%) of the upside. But that's only the beginning. The *true* magic comes from the annual reset.

Here's how it works. The interest rate the annuity pays you is tied to a market index, such as the S&P 500. Assume now that you started in an annuity when the S&P 500 was at 500, and the annuity has a 7% cap.

After year one it's at 550 for a 10% increase. This is reflected in the section marked "A" in the following illustration, also shown in the graph below. The investment starts a $100,000. The first green arrow (A) indicates a market gain of 10%. The FIA goes up by 7%, the full amount provided by the cap. The investment fund (market) went up by 8.9%, the amount of the index increase less the 1.1% fee.

During the second year (red arrow B in the illustration) the market fell by 10%. Now logically, the investment fund should be showing even, but remember there are fees charged...whether you make or lose money. Plus the 10% loss was on the full amount, not just the original $100,000. Therefore the investment fund is now in negative territory at $97,030.

However the FIA is still showing $107,000 due to the annual reset

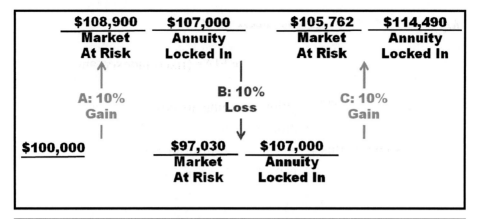

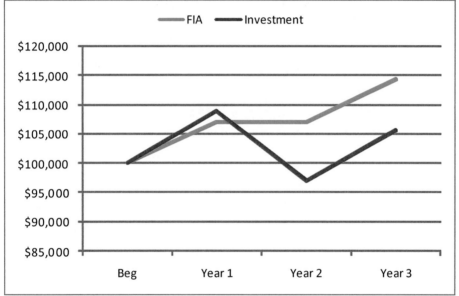

Figure 10: "Buy Low Sell High automated." These figures illustrate how FIAs differ from traditional investment funds when markets rise and fall. Note how on the FIA side, balances are locked in each year. That means that's the starting balance for the next year.

In order to lock in a position in the investment fund you must sell your position. So people have a tendency to "let it ride," a dangerous strategy in the market, but financial magic in the Fixed Indexed Annuity.

feature. Each year the interest accrued and the initial principal are "locked in." You can never go below that locked in amount!

So that's the first part of annual reset. Every year your principal and earnings are locked in and safe...they can never be taken away. But again, it's only the first part. There's another, even more powerful chapter to the story.

The actual index, in this case, the S&P 500, has lost 10%, so it's gone down to 495 (550 x .9 = 495). So with the investment fund, in order to get back to your high point, the S&P 500 must go back to 550 before you can recoup losses and start gaining from your high point. However on the FIA, the index has RESET. What's that mean.

Point one: all of your earnings and principal have been LOCKED IN at $107,000...it can never be less (as long as you don't withdraw money from the account and you honor the terms of the agreement).

Point two: the beginning point for the crediting of interest has been RESET to the current index level. In this case 495. That means any gains...any at all...from 495 get credited to your account...up to 7% (the cap)! This is financial magic.

Now take a look at Arrow C. See how the FIA has gained another 7%, fully compounded, to yield $114,490. The investment fund, however, is only at $105,762.

Looked at another way, you might even say that the FIA has taken the "buy low and sell high" principle and automated it for you! True, there is no buying and selling going on, but in effect that's what's happening. Each year that the market is up, you get to "lock in your position." Each year that the market is down, your principal and interest were protected, but the starting point was reset. Figure 11 is an actual illustration of one of my favorite FIAs compared to the S&P 500 and actual historical performance of CDs for the 10 year period beginning July 1, 1999. Notice

Sample Historical Performance (7/1/1999 - 7/1/2009)

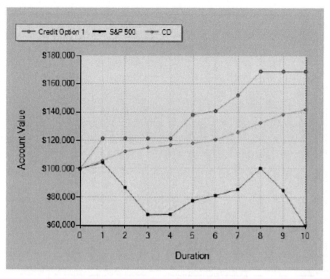

This chart illustrates how the Account Value changes at each anniversary over the specified time period. See the Statistical Analysis chart to view the performance over many historical time periods.

Figure 11: Safety First! Comparison of the Stock Market (red line), actual CD rates (the pink line) and Fixed Indexed Annuity for 10 year period beginning July 1, 1999.

how, by taking all of the market losses out of the equation, and annually resetting the begin balance and index starting point, the FIA significantly outperformed both CDs and the market.

All of the safety of a CD with market upside. It's a win all the way around!

No wonder Buffet said, "Rule number one is never lose your money, rule number two is never forget rule number one."

It is truly amazing to see the kinds of things we can do for people once risk, unnecessary fees, and taxes are taken out of the equation. We have helped people recoup losses and build solid financial futures with guaranteed income and security without the guesswork. If you have a better way...anywhere...take it.

Timing the Market vs. Time In the Market

I have talked to many people who have believed that the secret to success in the market has to do with "timing." I can tell you that in my experience, nothing is further from the truth. In fact, I defy you to show me anyone who can, with any accuracy, "time the market."

Certainly the preponderance of investors don't, including fund managers, retirement plan managers, and everyone else responsible for flows in and out of equity funds. If you need proof of this, you need look no further than this chart.

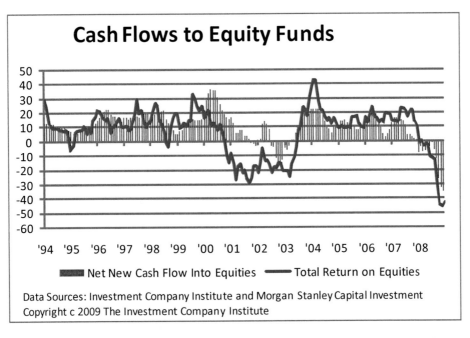

Figure 12: Comparison of cash flows into equity funds and fund performance from 1994-2008.

If investors were timing the market correctly, you would see cash inflows (the red bars) spiking and dipping BEFORE equity values (the blue line). In other words, money would flow into the market prior to stock values increasing (buy low), and would flow out of the market while stock values were still high, PRIOR to the dips (sell high). But as you can see, for the 14 year period from 1994 to 2008, it is exactly the opposite. People are buying late...after the market has already reached it high, and selling late, after the markets have crashed.

Bottom line: the vast majority of the money in the market is following it, not leading it. In other words the timing is way off...it's buying high and selling low.

This is because emotions are what triggers buying and selling. Here's how it normally goes (and the statistics...charts and data like that on the previous page...bear this out over and over again): People hear that the market is going up and up and people are making lots and lots of money. By the time they decide to get in, the market has already peaked (just look at the chart and you can see this is almost 100% true). So they pour their money in, hoping to take advantage. But now it's too late, and the market starts going down. But they've heard that you can't be faint of heart in the market, so they hold on and hold on and hold on until they just can't hold on any more. Then they sell...usually after losing a great deal. Once again, the chart bears that out.

This is what happens when people allow greed and fear to dictate their actions. And the vast majority of equity fund investors do just that.

In fact, we know that between 1984-2002, the S&P 500 had an annualized average return of 12.22%. However the average equity fund investor yielded only 2.57% during that time! Less taxes and fees! That's because the average length in a mutual fund was only two and one-half years!* People jumped in when the market was high (greed) and jumped out when they couldn't take it any more (fear). That's no way to manage your money!

* Source: Dalbar—Quantitative Analysis of Investor Behavior, ©2003

Bottom line: it's almost impossible to time the market. Those who say they can follow the paths of confidence men and shysters...just think of Bernie Madoff. It's almost always a scam. There is no such thing as a "safe" mutual fund. It's the same as a "safe" craps table.

In fact there are over 8,000 mutual funds in existence, all representing the same limited number of stocks, and over 6,000 of them do not beat the market. On average, it'd much better to just put your money into an index fund and hold on for dear life.

The problem of course, is that most people don't have the intestinal fortitude to do that. Who can blame them? When you see other people "becoming rich" (a fallacy, but nevertheless one that's hard to ignore) who can blame you for wanting to jump in? And then, when you see your hard-earned money going down the drain, who can blame you for getting out?

A Better Way

But what if there was a way? What if you could put your money in a very safe place...one that guaranteed you would never lose your principal or accrued interest? One that automatically "bought low" and "sold high"? One that encouraged you to stay in for enough time to ensure that you were able to enjoy the fruits of the market...but protected you from any and all downside? One that was tax-deferred and free of fees? One that returned all of your principal and earnings in the case of emergencies, death, etc., and provided excellent annual liquidity, penalty free? Further, one that could provide income guarantees for the rest of your life, ensuring up to 60% more income than could be had from any equity markets?

Wouldn't you be all over that? Well that's exactly what "Safe Harbor" Fixed Indexed Annuities do. The following illustration shows it in very simple terms.

Annual Reset in Action

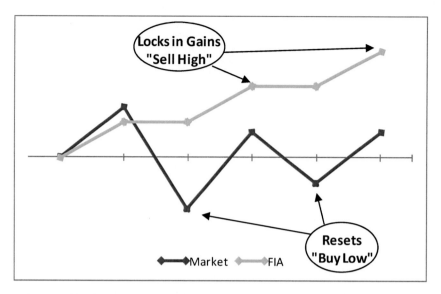

Figure 13: Demonstrates how an annual reset is like having your funds on auto pilot. When the market goes up, your gains are locked in. When it bottoms out, you can take advantage of the inevitable rebound.

When the market goes up (red line) so does the annuity (green line). When the market goes down, the annuity locks in gains and principal...never to be lost, essentially "selling high." When it goes up again, the annuity takes off from annual reset point, effectively "buying low." And since annuities are long-term strategies (1-10 years, depending on what you are looking for) they insure you are in the market long enough to benefit from the automated "Buy Low—Sell High" strategy.

Once again, however, they have excellent liquidity (10% or more per year without penalty...some as high as 100%!), and return all principal and interest in the event of catastrophic disease, long-term care, or death. In addition, many of them include income riders that provide for guaranteed income for the rest of your life without ever running out of money. All tax-deferred with virtually no fees.

They are a truly powerful tool for retirees and those getting ready to retire...one of the very best, in fact.

Smooth Sailing With A Lifetime Income!

Okay, now we've got the perfect product...or nearly perfect anyway. When the market is up, I am up, and when the market is down, I don't lose anything. But there's one catch...when the market is down I don't make anything either. I don't really like that scenario, especially since it requires that I tie up my money for a period of time. What can be done?

Well, imagine if you will a piece of paper with a line drawn down the middle. On the left side of the paper is the FIA, just as described in the preceding pages. But on the right side of the page you detail the following: An income account that's guaranteed to grow by no less than 5% per year (some as much as 8%), and when and if I need it, guaranteed to provide an income stream to me for the rest of my life...never running out of money. And it's the same product as the left side...just another option I can choose from. Oh, did I mention that if the left side outperforms the right side you get that benefit, too? Wow! Now that's a great idea.

Well, the insurance industry beat me to it, and over the last year a number of companies have created just such products. The following illustration shows how the "right side" works.

Assume you are 60 years old and are planning to retire at 70. You have $100,000 you want to put aside for income beginning at age 70. So you invest in a Fixed Indexed Annuity with an Income Option like the one shown above. By the time you are 70 the

Annuitant	◉ Single		5.0	% Premium Bonus
	○ Joint		60	Issue Age of Younger Annuitant (If Joint)
Initial Premium	100,000		120	Months of Deferral

Guaranteed Minimum Annual Payout

$12,626

Actual annual income may be higher.

Extended Details

Years Deferred	Attained Age	Income Acct. Value	Guaranteed Ann. Withdrawal	Confinement Benefit
0	60	$105,000	$5,250	$5,250
1	61	$112,560	$5,628	$11,256
2	62	$120,664	$6,033	$12,066
3	63	$129,352	$6,467	$12,934
4	64	$138,666	$6,933	$13,866
5	65	$148,649	$8,175	$16,350
6	66	$159,352	$8,764	$17,528
7	67	$170,826	$9,395	$18,790
8	68	$183,125	$10,071	$20,142
9	69	$196,310	$10,797	$21,594
10	70	$210,444	$12,626	$25,252

Figure 14: Best we've ever seen. Income Account doubles every 10 years and then guarantees income for life. But if you are confined to a nursing home it doubles for as long as you are confined.

income account (the right side of the paper) is guaranteed to have grown to $210,444 and yield a guaranteed income of $12,626 for the rest of your life. You can never run out of money!

But, if the market should take off, you still have the left side of the paper working for you! That means you could actually be making much more than 7% annually on your money. And if you are, that will be reflected on the income side as well! We call it having your cake and eating it, too!

Another important point is that you can turn income on and off any time, and still enjoy all the other benefits of the annuity. It is not necessary to annuitize the contract to get income! That is very, very powerful.

Most advisors use two well known rules of thumb to design a distribution plan for retirees. First, as far as investment is concerned, use the 100 minus your age formula for asset allocations. In other words, if you are 60, then 60% of your wealth should be in bonds, 40% in stocks.

The second part of the standard formula is that you should never take more than 4% of your wealth in annual payments. This is supposed to ensure that you never run out of money.

Wall Street calls this the Retirement Income Plan. I call it the R.I.P., or the "punt and pray" plan. Punt, based on artificial allocations, take a rate of payment low enough so you shouldn't run out of money, and then pray everything goes okay and that you don't, in fact, run out of money or build up too much surplus.

The problem is, taking 4%, or even 3% a year does not eliminate the possibility of running out of money, it merely reduces it. In fact the normal outcome of these two strategies is either a) running out of money, or b) creating giant surpluses for your heirs. Neither of which is optimal for you.

But don't take my word for it. William F. Sharpe, a developer of the Capital Asset Pricing Model which makes much of our modern day financial structure work, said about these plans, "Either the spending or investment rule can be part of an efficient strategy, but together they create either large surpluses or result in a failed spending plan."[1] Bottom line: the Holy Grail of Wall Street's Retirement Income Plan simply does not work well.

So then. Your choices seem to be using a tired and debunked model that has been based on two incompatible rules of thumb that the financial markets and Wall Street have a vested interest in promoting, or you can choose a plan that guarantees income for life, while allowing you to maximize gains without risk.

[1]Sharpe, William F., Scott, Jason S. and Watson, John G.,Efficient Retirement Financial Strategies(July 2007). Pension Research Council Working Paper Series. Available at SSRN: http://ssrn.com/abstract=1005652

Safe Harbor from Taxes

One of our most effective Safe Harbor Strategies is what we call "Income4Life" (I4L™) planning. This is a way of structuring your money that provides a planned income stream for the rest of your life, and also preserves a predetermined amount of your principal by utilizing the special benefits of insurance products.

To maximize your income you must have the ability to withdraw funds in a tax-advantaged manner. I4L™ planning <u>yields income that is between 50% and 93% tax-free</u>.

One of the key taxation issues is whether or not your income shows up in your provisional (threshold) income calculations when figuring Social Security taxes. CDs, mutual funds, other securities—<u>even tax-free bonds—all figure into your Social Security calculations</u>, and can cause you to pay more in taxes. If you find a strategy that does not, you can dramatically reduce your tax burden. Once again, tax deferred fixed annuities fit the bill.

Here's an example. We recently consulted with a retired couple who are in quite good shape with no debt, two homes, and have a substantial amount put away in pension and non-qualified accounts. Together they have Social Security of $19,800 and a pension of $18,000. They also have about $800,000 diversified in mutual funds, CDs, and tax-free bonds. These earn about $51,000 in income with about a 6% return.

They wanted to set aside money for their 3 young grandchildren's college tuition, but without impacting their lifestyle or future security. Leaving a family legacy was also a priority. And while they seemed in good shape, they were worried about running out of money.

Their money manager suggested they set aside money in a special "529 plan" for college tuition, but they were concerned about depleting their wealth and wanted to know if there was another way.

I4L™ planning using fixed annuities yielded a simple answer that their fee-based money manager missed. The mutual funds and CDs were fully taxable, and the tax-free bonds contributed to their provisional income for Social Security. This meant their Social Security was taxed at the maximum 85%. The net result was $75,000 in adjusted gross income and an annual Federal Income Tax bill of $7,784, as shown in Figure 15, below.

Figure 15: Tax return before I4L™ planning using fixed annuities

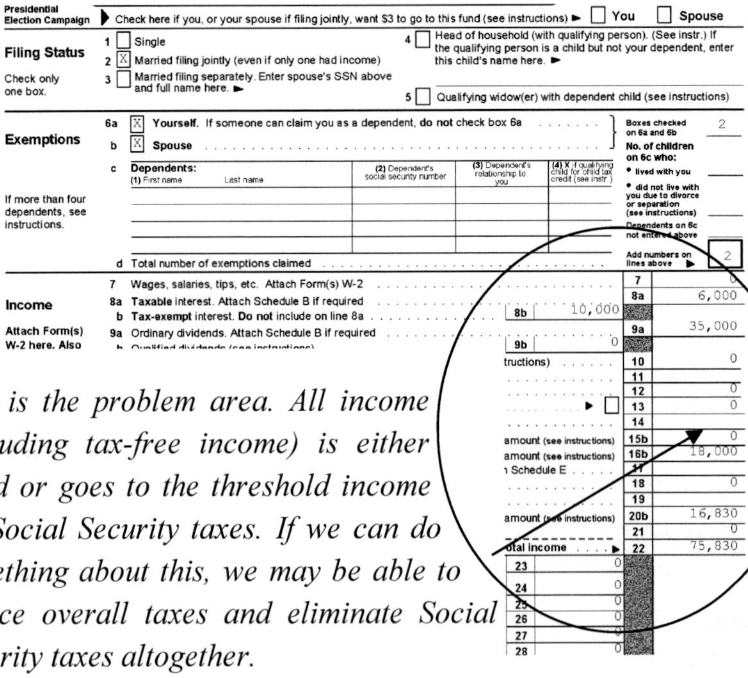

Presidential Election Campaign ▶ Check here if you, or your spouse if filing jointly, want $3 to go to this fund (see instructions) ▶ ☐ You ☐ Spouse

Filing Status
Check only one box.
1 ☐ Single
2 ☒ Married filing jointly (even if only one had income)
3 ☐ Married filing separately. Enter spouse's SSN above and full name here. ▶
4 ☐ Head of household (with qualifying person). (See instr.) If the qualifying person is a child but not your dependent, enter this child's name here. ▶
5 ☐ Qualifying widow(er) with dependent child (see instructions)

Exemptions
6a ☒ Yourself. If someone can claim you as a dependent, do not check box 6a
b ☒ Spouse
Boxes checked on 6a and 6b: 2
c Dependents: (1) First name Last name | (2) Dependent's social security number | (3) Dependent's relationship to you | (4) X if qualifying child for child tax credit (see instr.)
If more than four dependents, see instructions.
No. of children on 6c who: • lived with you • did not live with you due to divorce or separation (see instructions)
Dependents on 6c not entered above
d Total number of exemptions claimed — Add numbers on lines above ▶ 2

Income
Attach Form(s) W-2 here. Also
7 Wages, salaries, tips, etc. Attach Form(s) W-2 — 7: 0
8a Taxable interest. Attach Schedule B if required — 8a: 6,000
b Tax-exempt interest. Do not include on line 8a — 8b: 10,000
9a Ordinary dividends. Attach Schedule B if required — 9a: 35,000
9b: 0
10: 0
11
12: 0
13: 0
14
15b: 0
16b: 18,000
17
18: 0
19
20b: 16,830
21: 0
Total income ▶ 22: 75,830
23: 0
24: 0
25: 0
26: 0
27: 0
28: 0

This is the problem area. All income (including tax-free income) is either taxed or goes to the threshold income for Social Security taxes. If we can do something about this, we may be able to reduce overall taxes and eliminate Social Security taxes altogether.

By moving their mutual funds, CDs and tax-free bonds into an I4L™ plan using tax deferred fixed annuities with no fees, they were able to enjoy $39,060 in annual tax-free income. That reduced their provisional income level to $20,140, eliminating their Social Security tax, and reducing their Federal Income Tax to $204, without impacting their disposable income.

That freed up $7,580 every year to fund the 529 plan! It also ensured that their income would last as long as they lived and provide a family legacy long after they were gone.

Figure 16: Tax return after I4L™ plan using fixed annuities

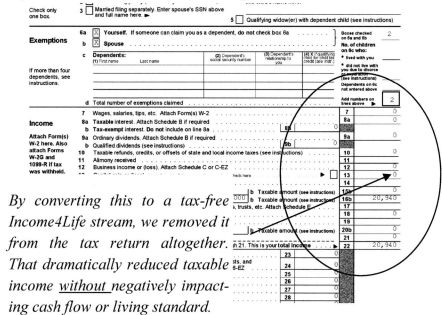

By converting this to a tax-free Income4Life stream, we removed it from the tax return altogether. That dramatically reduced taxable income *without* negatively impacting cash flow or living standard.

How can this be? Mutual funds and CDs generate annual taxes and fees, whether the money is used or reinvested. Since mutual funds have an average turnover of 110% annually, they are often taxed as ordinary income rather than long-term capital gains. And remember, mutual funds don't have to make money to be taxed...*in fact they can be taxed the most when they lose the most.*

Further, tax-free bonds also raise threshold income for Social Security taxes. Our client thought their bonds were tax-free! Well, you don't pay income taxes on any interest earned. But you do declare the interest on line 8b of your tax return (take a look on page 90), and it's used to calculate your tax liability. So, in effect, tax-free bonds are often not tax-free after all!

By creating an I4L™ plan using laddered and carefully managed tax deferred fixed annuities, our clients were able to dramatically reduce market risk, eliminate taxes, take a bite out of inflation, and help guarantee that they would never run out of money.

In addition, because of the favorable tax treatment, they were able to meet their commitments to their grandkids' college tuition without reducing their disposable income or savings!

Income4Life™ Calculator

Results	Income4Life	CDs	Enter your data here TAB Through the Cells	
	$0	$0	Desired Monthly Income:	$0
Initial Deposit:	$700,000	$700,000	Nest Egg/Initial Deposit:	$700,000
Recovery Balance:	$710,378	$402,556	Current Age:	65
Lost to Taxes & Interest:	$0	$451,723	Years to Delay Income (0-30)	0
Monthly Income:	$3,745	$2,809	Tax Rate:	0.25
Amount Tax Exempt:	$3,398	100% Taxed	Your Risk Tolerance:	Low
Add'l Annual Liquidity:	$49,139	$0	Adjust for Inflation?	No

The foundation of Income4Life™ Planning is principal preservation. After collecting income for 15 years, this plan provides for full recovery of the amount deposited, allowing you to start over again.

<<< CDs are inefficient Income4Life strategies. Note the $451,723 relative loss to taxes and fixed interest rates.

Figure 17: I4L™ Lifetime Income plan calculator

Who Really Owns Your IRA?

Side-bar: As a point of clarification, IRA is used as a reference to any tax-qualified dollars you put away for retirement. That can include IRAs, 401(k)s, pension plans, 403(b)s, etc.

Think for a moment about any asset you own…like a home, a life insurance policy, or a car. What are the rights you have that define your ownership?

First, any asset you claim ownership of is usually in your name. Take a look at the deed on your house, your life insurance policy, or the title on your car. Chances are you (or in some cases, a trust controlled by you) are listed as the owner. Now, look at your IRA (401(k), etc.). Who is named as the owner of that asset? You? Or is it some custodian or trustee you've never heard of (remember, YOU are the trustee of any trust you control).

The next right of ownership is the ability to KEEP the asset (there could be mitigating factors – such as eminent domain or bankruptcy – that may necessitate a sale, but when sold, you are entitled to fair market value for any property you are forced to liquidate). Are you allowed to keep your tax-qualified plan? No. First, it isn't even in your name (see above), and second the government dictates you must spend it all before you die – or at least before they say you will. (In fairness stretch IRAs extend that time limit, but the principle is the same).

The third right of ownership is the ability to sell your asset on the open market. Can you sell your IRA or 401(k)?

No, that is a federally prohibited transaction.

The fourth right of ownership is the ability to trade an asset for one of equal value. Again, you may not trade "your" tax-qualified plan. You cannot even give it away. These, too, are federally prohibited transactions.

Okay, so you can't have it in your name, you can't keep it, you can't sell it or trade it, and you can't give it away, but surely you can at least borrow against it, right? After all, it is an actual asset, right? No, that is also a federally prohibited transaction.

And we won't even talk about what happens if you have the bad form to die with it!

So do you REALLY own your IRA?

Today there are over six trillion dollars in assets in qualified plans. Want to know how big a trillion is? Recently my business partner's son asked him if he had lived a trillion seconds (the little squirt!). They sat down at his computer and determined that even as old as he looks, not only had my partner not lived a trillion seconds, but a trillion seconds has not yet passed since year one! In fact, a trillion seconds won't have passed until the year 31,709!

So Uncle Sam takes these assets very seriously and isn't about to give up his rights of ownership!

And the result is for every $100,000 in qualified funds, a minimum of $15,000 (and usually far more) in income taxes alone—not to mention estate taxes and state income taxes if applicable—will be paid by people who hold them or their heirs.

And if estate taxes do need to be paid, you can't pay those until you pay the income taxes!

Here's another thing to think about. When you made the deal with the IRS to defer taxes, you were essentially getting into a "pay me now or pay me later" bargain. As we all know, "pay me later" is almost always the losing deal.

Why? Because you didn't just defer the taxes, you deferred the tax rate as well. Now it was a good story that a lot of people bought. It went something like, "You're working full time now and in a higher tax bracket. Why not defer some taxes now and pay them later, when you are in a lower bracket?"

Sounds good, right? But that only tells a very small part of the story. Here's the part that wasn't mentioned:

First, the deal you made was to pay the taxes not on the SEED, but on the HARVEST. This is a great deal for Uncle Sam, but maybe not so much for you. Just do the math; would you rather get a tax deduction on $2,000-$6,000 per year or get tax-free income of $25,000-$30,000 per year all during your retirement? Exactly.

Second, after you are retired, when your tax rate presumably has gone down, you no longer typically have certain tax deductions you have when you are younger. Deductions like a home mortgage, health care, etc., etc. So sometimes your rate hasn't gone down at all.

Third, let's attack the "lower tax bracket" argument at its core. Do you really believe taxes are going to be lower as time goes on? Think about it. We are currently running deficits of over a trillion dollars a year, healthcare and Social Security are about to implode, we are spending billions on two wars that have no conceivable end in sight, billions more rescuing whole industries, and we have just suffered the worst economic downturn since the Great Depression. Do you really think taxes are going to go down?

Really?

So where does that leave you? Did you know that some people pay as much as 66% in taxes on their qualified money? That's right, the government can take up to 66% of your IRA, 401(k), 403(b) or other qualified retirement plans! That leaves you and your heirs just 34% of the savings you have worked your lifetime to accumulate!

I can't tell you how many times people have told me they are taking part of their retirement money because Uncle Sam says "they have to." They have to? What's that about? Your money should be something you take out because you want to, or need to...not because the government makes you!

So what are some of the strategies you can use in order to avoid paying some of these taxes? A dirty little secret is many advisors don't know! So they tell you to spend your already taxed money and push your qualified money onto your kids so *they* can worry about the taxes.

Let's look at this. You worked hard all your life and put as much money as you could afford into your qualified plan, because your advisor told you to. And now you're in retirement, and the best advice you can get is, "Don't spend it so you don't have to pay taxes on it," often from the same person who told you to put it away!

So knowing all of this, is there anything you can do about it? Well, maybe. In order to find out, like anything else, you have to crunch the numbers (that's where your advisor comes in).

There are three general strategies we often use: Roth It, Stretch It or Insure it...or a combination of the three.

Insure It With An IPA

One of our favorite strategies is one we call an Individual Pension Account (IPA™). This one comes under the "Insure It" category. **It lets you take a maximum amount of income while you are alive, and leave 100% of your IRA to your heirs...tax free!**

As we mentioned earlier, taxes on qualified money can be as much as 66% . The primary taxes are Estate and Inheritance Taxes, Income Taxes, and Income Taxes In Respect to the Decedent (IRD). That last is a fancy way of saying that if you don't pay the taxes while you are alive, your children will have to after you are gone. And most often, at a higher rate. You can offset the IRD and Inheritance Taxes against each other, so be sure to take that up with your advisor.

So how does the IPA™ help?

Consider the example on the next page. Assume your IRA is worth $250,000 and you are 70 ½ years old, and you are now forced to take the required minimum distribution (RMD), whether you want it or not. You may not realize that if you abide by the RMD tables as mandated by federal tax statute, you will be forced to take the most income at age 93 when you are apt to need it the least. Then, when you do finally pass it along to your heirs, they will be forced to pay taxes on their inheritance (and it can also raise the stakes for any other death taxes you may incur).

The first section in the calculator shows the impact of the IPA™ after year one. Income with the Required Minimum Distribution (RMD) is $9,124, but the IPA™ provides $14,764 (61% more). If death occurred now, $250,000 goes to heirs, but under the traditional IRA, there is an IRD tax of $93,431 plus any inheritance or estate taxes. However under the IPA™, that money passes free of all taxes. So the IPA™ is immediately worth almost 60% more.

At life expectancy—age 82—RMDs have risen to $13,736. Since age 70, the IPA™ has provided about $44,000 more in income.

Figure 18: IPA™ (a.k.a. IRA 590™) plan compared to traditional IRA

Individual Pension Account (IPA™) Calculator

Enter Your Age:	70	Enter your age, the amount of your qualified funds, and your sex. The calculator will show you the impact an IRA 590™ could have on your retirement.	
Enter the Size of Your IRA:	$250,000		
Your Sex:	Male		

	Traditional IRA	Income4Life IRA 590™	Advantage or Disadvantage
Year One			
Annual Income:	$9,124	$14,764	**61.81%** — More income now and guaranteed for life with the IRA 590™
Death Benefit:	$250,000	$250,000	**100.00%** — Equal amounts go to heirs at the beginning of withdrawals
Tax paid by heirs:	$93,431		**$93,431** — More goes to heirs. The IRA 590™ passes to heirs completely tax free.
To Heirs After Tax:	$156,569	$250,000	**59.67%** — More value from the very beginning!
Life Expectancy Age 82			
Annual Income:	$13,736	$14,764	**7.48%** — More income continues to be generated by the IRA 590™ for life.
Total Income Received:	$147,961	$191,932	**29.72%** — More income received since income began.
Death Benefit:	$234,886	$250,000	**6.43%** — More to heirs, because the IRA 590™ is never drawn down by distributions.
Tax paid by heirs:	$91,139		**$91,139** — More to heirs on the IRA 590™. The IRA 590™ passes to heirs completely tax free.
Net Death Benefit:	$143,748	$250,000	**73.92%** — More since the IRA 590™ passes completely tax free to heirs.
Total Benefits:	$291,709	$441,932	**51.50%** — More at life expectancy. In fact, the longer you live, the more valuable it becomes.

Net to Heirs: Even More if Inheritance Taxes Apply

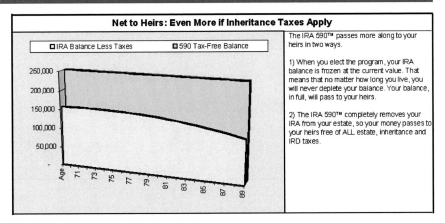

The IRA 590™ passes more along to your heirs in two ways.

1) When you elect the program, your IRA balance is frozen at the current value. That means that no matter how long you live, you will never deplete your balance. Your balance, in full, will pass to your heirs.

2) The IRA 590™ completely removes your IRA from your estate, so your money passes to your heirs free of ALL estate, inheritance and IRD taxes.

IPA™ is a trademark of Consolpro™. The plan is only available through Consolpro™ and its agents. Any numbers used in this calculator and illustrations within this book are deemed accurate but are for illustration purposes only.

But because the IPA™ is an Income4Life principal preservation strategy, the death benefit is still $250,000, where the IRA has been depleted to $234,866. In addition, the IPA™ passes to heirs completely tax-free, instead of the $91,139 in IRD taxes paid on the traditional IRA. Therefore, the $250,000 is worth $135,000 more in the IPA™ than the traditional IRA in only 12 years, GUARANTEED, without increasing risk at all.

Once again, it's not what you make but what you keep that matters. And it's not magic; it's simply managing risk, fees and taxes that makes the difference.

Like any pension plan, the IPA™ can be configured many ways. It can include a long term care benefit, health insurance, life insurance...any benefit you want. And the best part about it is that if you do it right, it never costs a dime. How? By utilizing the dollars you would have paid to Uncle Sam in taxes to fund the plan!

Roth It

Another alternative is to convert your IRA or other qualified funds to a Roth IRA. A Roth IRA has many of the advantages of a traditional IRA, only better.

A traditional IRA allows you to grow your money tax-deferred. That provides a great advantage to you, because it allows you to earn interest on the government's money. Ultimately, though, you must pay the tax when you withdraw the money.

But what if, instead of tax deferred, you could grow your money tax free? So not only was your principal tax free, but the entire balance of your money...principal and interest...were tax free? That's exactly what a Roth IRA does for you.

This can provide many advantages to you when you are in retirement. First, 100% of the money you take out is tax-free. No taxes at all. But equally as important, Roth distributions are not reported on your income tax return, so they also don't raise your income threshold for Social Security taxes (unlike income from a traditional IRA). Also, they can be passed, income tax free, to your heirs when you die.

So why doesn't everyone just convert their IRAs to a Roth and be done with it?

There are several reasons. The first, and most obvious reason, is that when you convert your qualified money to an IRA, it's the same as withdrawing it from your account. And when you withdraw it, you must pay taxes on it. For many people, this is an insurmountable barrier.

Another reason is that there have been income restrictions on Roth conversions. Traditionally, individuals or joint filers needed a modified adjusted gross income (MAGI) of less than $100,000 to qualify for a Roth conversion. But new legislation, effective January 1, 2010, lift those restrictions, enabling higher-income investors to convert. However, income limits remain in effect for new contributions, and Congress may decide to reinstate the old income limits or impose new ones at any time. So basically this is a great, and possibly fleeting, opportunity for many people.

If you believe your tax rate is currently lower than it will be in the future there may be a significant advantage to paying taxes on your IRA assets now.

You should also be aware that income and tax liability for a conversion made in 2010 can be spread out equally, in a one-time allowance, over 2011 and 2012.

So how do the numbers work?

Here's an actual example of a case I recently had. The couple, call them Jack and Jill Hill, came in with a number of qualified accounts, IRAs, 401(k)s and 403(b)s in the amount of $500,000, and they were looking for a way to maximize the payout on these funds. Jill was 66 and Jack was 62. So we looked at a Roth conversion to see if it made sense.

The first thing we had to calculate was what the taxes would be. Since their adjusted gross income was around $92,000 and they were married, filing jointly, Jack and Jill's income tax bracket was 25%. That meant that converting the traditional IRA to a Roth would cost them $125,000 in taxes! Could it possibly make sense to do that?

One of the things we have available in Fixed Indexed Annuities that is unavailable anywhere else are contracts that provide up to a 12% bonus, guaranteed, for all initial deposits. That meant that almost half of the taxes could be paid with a tax-free bonus of $60,000, leaving only $65,000 left to pay.

Another consideration is whether to pay the taxes from the IRA funds or from separate funds. Whenever possible, it is better to pay with outside funds. Why? Because the money in the Roth is worth more than the money outside the Roth since it can grow tax-free. So, if we pay the tax from outside funds, we have less money outside the Roth but that much more inside. In this case the difference is $185,000 in tax-free dollars. Before the conversion they had $500,000 in totally untaxed dollars and about $250,000 in normal, taxed (non-Roth) dollars. Now that was okay, but every dollar they made from investing both types of dollars would be taxed, as well as all money taken from the IRA.

So, this was the picture before the conversion:

$250,000 Non-qualified savings and investments (all available for spending without paying taxes, but any growth would be taxed).

$500,000 Qualified savings. 100% taxable when withdrawn. Growth tax-deferred but ultimately taxable, requires minimum distribution, raises Social Security taxes, and huge potential taxes when passed to heirs.

Now, assume retirement when Jack turns 70 with a 6% average growth rate, and both live to life expectancy: Jack 82, Jill 88.

At 6% growth, the IRA grows to $796,924 by age 70. If they take a conservative 4% in income beginning at age 70, income starts at around $32,000 per year and grows to about $42,000 at age 82, providing an inflation hedge. However taxes take a 25% bite out of the income, reducing annual income, and there is about a 40% tax bite at death. Resulting value, including the taxable growth of the original non-qualified $250,000 and net of taxes: $1,652,572.

Now the Roth conversion, taking the taxes out of the non-qualified $250,000. Immediately on conversion we have $125,000 non-qualified, and $560,000 Roth money. This is where it gets fun.

Now the TAX FREE income from the Roth begins a $35,065 at age 70 and ends up at $44,766 at 82. Net income was $596,000 instead of $451,000. No IRD taxes to heirs; they get the full balance at death (less any estate taxes). Total net value, including the growth on the non-qualified $125,000 net of taxes: $1,980,288.

That's an increase of over $325,000, just for converting to the Roth. And it also freed Jack and Jill to spend their money without worrying about it; it was income tax free and at death they passed almost $1.4 million to their heirs, also income tax free! Plus, they had 32% more income to spend while alive, and it helped keep their Social Security taxes down. It was a win all the way around. All with no risk and no fees! So you may wish to discuss a Roth conversion with someone who really understands them.

Figure 19: Results of Roth Conversion vs. Traditional IRA

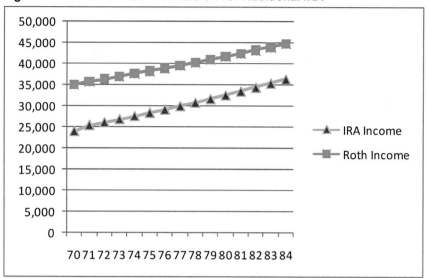

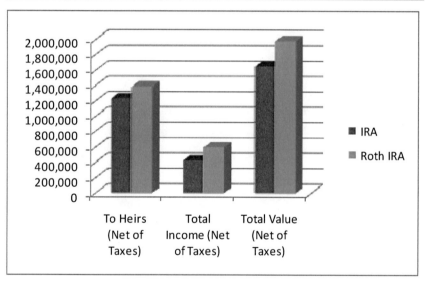

Stretch It

You can net even more out of your IRA by using a "Stretch" or "Multi-Gen" IRA. Combined with a Roth conversion, this strategy can save hundreds of thousands of dollars in taxes. Here's how it works.

The IRS allows your children and grandchildren to "step into" your IRA as if it were their own, and take the distributions over their several life spans. This means a few hundred thousand dollars can ultimately be worth several million, if handled correctly.

Take the previous case of Jack and Jill. Jack and Jill have three children, Larry, Moe and Joe; 42,38,and 40, respectively. They in turn, have four children among them. Average age of all of Jack and Jill's offspring (children and grandchildren): 23 years old.

Just doing a rough estimate based on the 6% return assumed for Jack and Jill, converting to a Roth IRA, and stretching it over a lifespan starting at age 23, the difference in value for the Hill family of stretching the initial $500,000 over three generations:

Figure 20: Impact of stretching Roth and Traditional IRAs

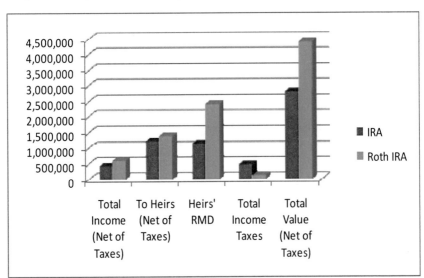

Either way, it should be clear that stretching the IRA, whether a Traditional IRA or a Roth, is a prudent thing to do. The problem associated with doing so are complicated however.

First, before anything else, you have to have your IRA money with a custodian that will allow your beneficiaries to stretch. That's right; some banks and fund managers WILL NOT ALLOW your IRA to be stretched: they require it all be taken within one to five years, thus cheating your offspring out of potentially millions in benefits.

Second, there are two very important technical details that must be handled if the IRA monies are to be stretched: proper beneficiary designations, and proper account setups. Without these two details handled very carefully, all of you heirs might have to stretch the IRA based on the age of the eldest sibling, thus cheating the younger siblings and their children out of potentially tens of thousands in benefits.

In my office we have very sophisticated computer software that is designed specifically to determine if converting a traditional IRA to a Roth, or stretching either kind over multiple generations, makes sense for each individual's case. We would be happy to run illustrations for you to determine if either of the strategies is in your best interest. Simply contact us using the information at the back of this book.

Long Term Care:
Navigating "de Nile" River

This is a difficult subject for many people because they just really don't want to think about it: What happens if you need long term care or you need to go into a nursing home?

I've heard every kind of answer. Some people have told me it would never happen to them (how they know, I couldn't tell you). Others tell me their kids will take care of them. I had one tell me recently that he was going to get into his boat, motor 20 miles off shore, and jump in!

There is one common theme to all of these answers. They are all examples of a river in Egypt.

Others tell me Medicare will take care of them. Wrong! Medicare DOES NOT PAY FOR NURSING HOME CARE. If an advisor tells you this, it's time to get another advisor.

Medicare will pay for a limited amount of skilled nursing care if,

• You are RECOVERING from an illness or injury,

• You were in a hospital for at least three nights for the same condition.

If and when you are no longer recovering, i.e., actively improving your condition, Medicare stops paying.

Nursing care, under the auspices of Long Term Care, is classified as CUSTODIAL CARE. This means that your condition is not improving. Either it is staying the same, or getting worse.

Now I understand that people really don't want to think about this subject. It's unpleasant. It's much more pleasant to avoid altogether. And it isn't going to happen for years and years.

Wrong again! Age is not an issue with long term care. What is an issue is the denial that over half of us will need some long term care in our lives. That could mean you or your spouse, or both.

How well prepared are you today if something happened tomorrow? It may be too late to get insurance if you already have health issues. There is a truth in my business every good agent knows— you don't buy insurance with money, you buy it with your health.

Here are the facts:

- 40% of persons receiving long term care are between 18 and 64.

- Over 50% of the population will need long term care sometime in their lifetime. That means if you are single, you have a one in two chance of needing care. If you are married, the statistical probability that one of you will need care goes to 100%!

- Often it is a woman's issue. More than half of all women and a third of all men will spend time in a nursing home.

- There is competition for the government funded beds. If you are on Medicaid and need to go to a nursing home the closest bed available may be some distance from your family and friends.

- Medicaid will pay for care, but it is welfare, and you must first liquidate and spend down virtually everything you own in order to qualify. The fact is that Medicaid IS BY FAR THE MOST EXPENSIVE way to fund long term care.

Few of us are willing to accept that we will likely need any long term care. Most of us are in denial that we will ever need assistance with eating, dressing, bathing, toileting, or moving about.

Denial can be a mask for fear. But if we don't face our fear and make plans the consequences to our selves and our families can be devastating.

Are you assuming that your adult children will take care of you? Family members will find it difficult to provide an adequate level of care, even though they will likely want to try.

In most cases the burden falls on the daughter, or daughter-in-law. If the latter, is it really fair to place the burden of your care on the wife of your son? How would that impact their marriage? And how would taking care of you effect their families and jobs?

If your spouse or family cannot take care of you, can you or they afford to pay for your care? Is it fair to expect them to?

Like many risks whose consequences effect everyone around us it's all a matter of if you are willing to take responsibility for yourself.

According to experts, <u>leaving yourself uninsured for long term care is more risky than if you were to cancel your health insurance, homeowners insurance, and car insurance</u>. But statistics are for the other guy, not me...right?

When you overcome your denial about your long term care risk and recognize the consequences that your long term care will have on your family and friends, then you are ready to decide if you should continue to self-insure or transfer the financial burden to an insurance company just like you do for the risks to your health, home, and car.

And the costs of transferring that risk can be less than you think. In fact, if you were to use an Individual Pension Account (see page 97), chances are you may be able to fund it with tax dollars.

<u>If so, it could very well be free, or nearly so, for you.</u>

There are other things to consider. For most people, the thought of ending up in a nursing home is the most abhorrent thing they can think of. People want to remain in their homes and be surrounded by their loved ones!

If you want to remain in your home, and you need someone to help you get around, bathe, toilet yourself, etc., how are you going to do it without having someone come in? Do you really think you or your children would be happy if they were the ones providing these services? Don't you want your relationship with them to be so much more dignified and less stressful?

But home health care is expensive, and with rare exceptions Medicaid does not underwrite this type of care. Medicaid pays almost exclusively for nursing care. So if you are relying on Medicaid to provide these services, you are planning to end up in the place you least want to be.

Today's long term care plans are designed to keep you in your home as long as possible. They provide funds for in home care, installation of ramps, stairway lifts, rails, etc. They give you day care benefits. They make sure you are able to stay where you want, for as long as you can, with dignity.

And you might be surprised as to what one of today's policies look like. For example how about a policy that:

- Covered all of your needs if you should require care at home, in a facility, or both...but,

- Gave you 100% of your money back any time you like...all you have to do is ask for it?

- Gave you 100% of your money back, plus interest, if you died without needing care?

Here's an actual example of a case we just completed for a 71 year old client who had several hundred thousand sitting in CDs. His thought was that it was money set aside for his children and grandchildren.

When we first started talking about long term care he didn't even want to discuss it because he figured it was a waste of money. "Besides," he said, "Medicare pays for it." But after I explained to him that, "Medicare does not pay...Medicaid does, and that's welfare, and it only pays after you have gone through all your money, including what you wanted to give to your grandchildren," he was much more willing to talk.

Ultimately we diverted $100,000 of his CD money into a policy that would provide a $335,000 pool of LTC money, available over a six year period at about $4,500 per month for long-term care services including adult day care, home health care, personal care services, hospice services, nursing home care services, assisted living, and alternative care services. However, if he were to die and hadn't used it, $110,000 would be paid to his grandchildren...and if at any time he wanted to get his money back, all he had to do was ask for it.

At the end of that conversation, after we had it all in place, he confessed to me how much better he felt, and he thanked me for pressing the issue. He told me he'd always worried about what he would do if he needed care...but he couldn't bring himself to spending money on insurance.

This could be one of the most important decisions you make for your own sake and those you leave behind. Don't you think you owe it to them (and yourself!) to at least have a frank discussion with someone about it?

What could you possibly have to lose (except everything you own, if you don't?).

Are Safe Harbors for Everyone?

We believe life insurance and annuities belong in most financial plans. But of course there are always exceptions.

These Safe Harbors are medium to long-term, low-risk, semi-liquid, tax-deferred strategies without fees.

Anyone who needs to keep all their assets fully liquid in the short term may not want them tied up. Likewise, anyone who is less risk-averse, has enough wealth and existing life insurance, and is willing to speculate in the market in the face of risk, fees and taxes may not want to put their money in these Safe Harbors.

Life insurance and annuities are for those who want to let their nest egg accumulate safely over time, participate in market gains, and take the maximum amount of income without risking principal, or paying fees and taxes. They are also very important for people with large estates that have estate tax issues.

If that describes you, these strategies might just be the way to go.

Made in the USA
San Bernardino, CA
05 May 2016